Health Financing in the Republic of Gabon

A WORLD BANK STUDY

Health Financing in the Republic of Gabon

Karima Saleh, Bernard F. Couttolenc, and Helene Barroy

Contents

Boxes

Figures

Foreword

This book is a comprehensive assessment of health financing in the Republic of Gabon. The book reviews the health financing situation in light of the government's introduction of a national health insurance program and its commitment to achieving universal health insurance coverage in the medium term. The book provides a diagnostic of the situation in light of recent data from the demographic and health survey, updated national health accounts, and a review of public expenditures in the health sector. Additionally, it performs a benchmarking exercise to assess how Gabon performs in its health spending and health outcomes compared to countries of similar income and compared to countries in the region. A forthcoming household survey is expected to provide better information on financial protection against illness costs.

Universal health coverage has been defined as a situation where all people who need health services (prevention, promotion, treatment, rehabilitation, and palliative) receive them without undue financial hardships (World Health Report 2010). Universal health coverage consists of three interrelated components: (i) a need-based full spectrum of quality health services; (ii) financial protection from direct payments for health services when consumed; and (iii) coverage for the entire population. This book attempts to diagnose Gabon's current situation in regards to achieving universal health coverage. Gabon should be commended for its commitment to improving health indicators of the poor and the underserved.

The book shows that while the government has set an ambitious goal for itself, several challenges exist in meeting these objectives in the medium term. Resource mobilization efforts are a priority to sustain its programs financially; to prioritize resources for areas considered "value for money," to improve equity in access and delivery of health services, with particular focus on primary care, public health program, and quality of care; to increase the population's coverage under the national health insurance program, with focus on the poor and the informal sector workers; and to consider areas that would improve efficiency and reduce costs.

The book is timely, given that the government has recently produced "the Plan Social." It provides a diagnostic of the health sector and provides key recommendations—options for the government to consider in the short to medium term.

Gregor Binkert
Country Director
Angola, Cameroon, Central Africa Republic,
Gabon, Equatorial Guinea, and São Tomé and Principe

Acknowledgments

This task has been led by Karima Saleh, Senior Economist (Health), and task team leader, from the Health, Nutrition and Population Department of the West and Central Africa Region (AFTHW), World Bank. Other team members included Bernard Couttolenc (Consultant, AFTHW) and Helene Barroy (Economist, HDNHE). Others who provided inputs include Lombe Kasonde (Operations Analyst, HDNHE), who provided research assistance; Alejandro Ramos, Montserrat Meiro Lorenzo, and Roberto Iglesias (HDNHE), who supplied information on tobacco taxes; Hui Wang (Junior Professional Associate, HDNHE), who helped run regressions and simulations; Sariette Jippe (Program Assistant, AFTHW), who offered administrative support; and Susan Middaugh, who provided editorial support. The authors are grateful to the following for their valuable feedback, which benefitted the book. Peer reviewers included Ajay Tandon, Rick Emery Tsouck Ibounde, John Langenbrunner, Moulay Driss Zine Eddine El Idrissi, and Netsanet Workie. Tawhid Nawaz also made comments. The team is grateful to Ritva Reinikka (former HD Sector Director, AFTHD) and Trina Haque (HNP Sector Manager, AFTHW) for their support. The team would also like to thank the Bank's Country Management Unit (Gregor Binkert, Country Director; Zouera Youssoufou, Gabon Country Manager; and Olivier Godron, Country Program Coordinator) for providing the team this opportunity and a budget to go with it.

The team is grateful to the Government of Gabon for its cooperation. The team appreciated the support and information shared with them during their mission to Gabon in November 2012 and July 2013. Special appreciation goes to Dr. Jean Damascene Khouilla, Director General of Ministry of Health and Public Hygiene (MOHPH). We are also grateful for valuable discussions held with others at the MOHPH; the Director General, Deputy Director General and team at the Caisse Nationale d'Assurance Maladie et de Garantie Sociale (CNAMGS); and the Director of the Budget and staff at the Ministry of Economy. The team visited several health facilities in and outside of Libreville and very much appreciated the cooperation and open discussion they encountered during those visits. The team also benefited from discussions with the staff of the World Health Organization in Gabon.

About the Authors

Karima Saleh is a Senior Health Economist at the World Bank. She has nearly 20 years of experience working in more than 15 countries, with work experience (including fieldwork) on health financing and service delivery policy and planning in low- and lower-middle-income countries. She holds a PhD in health economics from the Johns Hopkins University, United States. She was part of the core team that developed the *World Development Report 1993: Investing in Health* (World Bank 1993). Among her recent publications are *The Health Sector in Ghana: A Comprehensive Assessment* (World Bank 2013) and *Health Financing in Ghana* (World Bank 2012).

Bernard F. Couttolenc is Chief Executive Officer of the Performa Institute, a new policy research center in São Paulo, Brazil. He has a master's degree in business management and a PhD in health economics from the Johns Hopkins University, United States. He has worked for many years in executive positions in public and private hospitals in Brazil as well as in planning and financing of the public health system. He has nearly 20 years of experience consulting with international organizations. For more than 10 years, he held a teaching position at the University of São Paulo, where he conducted research in health economics, financing, and economic evaluation. He has authored several publications.

Helene Barroy is a Health Economist at the World Bank. Prior to this she worked as a health financing adviser for the French Government; a lecturer at the Master of International Affairs at Sciences Po; and an expert providing technical support on health and health financing reforms and has led health operations over 10 years in over 10 countries. She holds an MSc in public health from the London School of Hygiene and Tropical Medicine and a PhD in health economics from the CERDI, France. Among her recent publications are *Sustaining UHC in France: A Perpetual Challenge* (World Bank 2014) and *Vietnam and UHC: Learning from Smart Reforms* (World Bank 2014).

Abbreviations

AIDS	acquired immune deficiency syndrome
ARI	acute respiratory infection
ART	antiretroviral therapy
BMI	Business Monitor International
CEMAC	The Economic Community of Central African States
CHR	Regional Hospitals (Centres Hospitaliers Régionaux)
CHU	Centre Hospitalier Universitaire
CNAMGS	National Health Insurance and Social Security (Caisse Nationale d'Assurance Maladie et de Garantie Sociale)
CNGS	Health Insurance Scheme for the Poor (Caisse Nationale de Garantie Sociale)
CNSS	Social Security Scheme (Caisse Nationale de Securité Sociale)
COSP	Monitoring Unit for Public Health, Ministry of Health (Cellule d'Observation de la Santé Publique)
CSMBS	Civil Servant Medical Benefit Scheme
DOTS	directly observed treatment, short-course (for tuberculosis)
DRS	regional health directorates
EGEP	Enquête Gabonaise sur l'Evaluation et le suivi de la Pauvreté
FCTC	Framework Convention on Tobacco Control (of the World Health Organization)
FHP	Family Health Program
GDHS	Gabon Demographic Health Survey
GDP	gross domestic product
GEF	Fund for the Poor (Gabonais Economiquement Faibles)
GGHE	general government health expenditure
GHS	government health spending
GIS	geographical information systems
GNI	gross national income
GPRS	Growth Poverty Reduction Strategy

GPRSP	Growth and Poverty Reduction Strategy Paper
HDI	human development index
HIAOBO	Hopital d'Instruction des Armées Omar Bongo Ondimba
HIV	human immunodeficiency virus
ICT	information and communication technology
IGR	internally generated revenue
IMF	International Monetary Fund
IMR	infant mortality rate
L'OPN	National Pharmaceutical Procurement Office (L'Office Pharmaceutique National)
MDG	Millennium Development Goal
MOHPH	Ministry of Health and Public Hygiene
MONP	temporary/contractual workers budget line item (agents de la main d'oeuvre non)
MMR	maternal mortality ratio
NCU	national currency unit
NGO	nongovernmental organization
NHA	National Health Accounts
NHIP	National Health Insurance Program
NHS	National Health Services
NTD	neglected tropical diseases
ODA	Official Development Assistance
OECD	Organization for Economic Cooperation and Development
OOP	out-of-pocket
ORT	oral rehydration therapy
PEC	*prises en charge*
PETS	Public Expenditure Tracking Survey
PHC	primary health care
PNDS	National Health Development Plan
PPP	purchasing power parity
RBF	results-based financing
ROAM	levies for the poor (Redevance Obligatoire à l'Assurance Maladie)
ROI	return on investment
SSA	Sub-Saharan Africa
SSS	Social Security Scheme
TB	tuberculosis
THE	total health expenditure
U5MR	under-5 mortality rate

UAE	United Arab Emirates
UCS	universal coverage scheme
UMIC	upper-middle-income country
UNDP	United Nations Development Program
UNICEF	United Nations Children's Fund
UNFPA	United Nations Population Fund
VAT	value added tax
WDI	World Development Indicators
WHO	World Health Organization
WHO-JLN	World Health Organization and Joint Learning Network
XAF	Central Africa CFA Francs (currency)

All dollar amounts are U.S. dollars unless otherwise indicated.

Executive Summary

Background

This is a review of the health financing situation in the Republic of Gabon. The book reviews the situation in the country under the lens of the principles of health financing: revenue mobilization for health, risk pooling, and purchasing services. The book also estimates the fiscal space in health, that is, looking at options that could increase resources for health within a macroeconomic and fiscal context.

Universal health coverage has been defined as a situation where all people who need health services (prevention, promotion, treatment, rehabilitation, and palliative) receive them, without undue financial hardship (World Health Report 2010). Universal health coverage consists of three inter-related components: (i) the full spectrum of quality health services according to need; (ii) financial protection from direct payment for health services when consumed; and (iii) coverage for the entire population.

Because of Gabon's commitment to universal health coverage, certain segments are calling for additional resources for this sector. As a result, the country is grappling with the following (i) how are resources being spent, (ii) is there room for a more efficient allocation of current resources or (iii) is there an urgent need to mobilize additional resources to meet this goal. This book attempts to diagnose the situation and offer additional information to enlighten and fuel the debate.

Positive Developments in Gabon's Path to Universal Health Coverage

The Ministry of Health and Public Hygiene (MOHPH) has prepared a National Health Development Plan 2011–15 (Republic of Gabon, Ministry of Health and Public Hygiene 2010), that has committed to achieve universal health coverage. Having undertaken various health finance reforms over the years—ranging from user fees to free health care under a national health service—Gabon launched the national health insurance program (NHIP) in 2007 under the Caisse Nationale d'Assurance Maladie et de Garantie Sociale (National Health Insurance and Social Security; CNAMGS), and aims to achieve universal insurance coverage.

Since the introduction of the NHIP, the country has redirected its resources in favor of demand-side financing[1] and earmarked funds for health. Because of the government's objective to achieve universal health coverage, public sector resources doubled in per capita nominal terms from $100 to $200 between 2008 and 2012. Moreover, the percentage of total health spending dedicated to the public sector increased from 40 percent in 2008 to 51 percent in 2012. Budget allocations for health increased to 7.2 percent by 2012, and as much as 27 percent of public financing gets allocated to the NHIP. This is a huge undertaking.

It is normal to see public financing rise as a country moves toward covering a larger segment of its population with publicly funded health services and goods. Indeed, public financing is often critical for countries that have a significant population living below the poverty level and for countries with a small segment of its population working in the formal sector. Commitment for resources and sustainability of public financing will be critical to achieving universal health coverage. The NHIP—a comprehensive program for all the people of Gabon— began enrolling the poor and has fully subsidized their premiums from general and earmarked taxes and levies. Later, other subgroups within the population also enrolled, but their premium contributions derive from private contributions through payroll taxes. However, the mandatory scheme for the informal sector is not yet introduced.

As of 2012, 45 percent of the population was covered by the NHIP. The NHIP emphasized solidarity and inclusiveness. The poor were the primary focus of the program and the first group to be covered. The NHIP claims to have achieved universal coverage among this subgroup. Gabon deserves to be commended for doing so. However, a significant population does not have a compulsory program, and this population belongs to the informal sector. Their inclusion will be critical to achieving universal health insurance coverage.

The NHIP is beneficial as long as people remain enrolled in the program and as long as the package of services and drugs address the health needs of its beneficiaries. Gabon offers a comprehensive benefit package under the NHIP, and that which complements benefits provided by the MOHPH. NHIP contracts both public and private providers within their benefits package.

The government has attempted to improve access to and quality of health care and injected resources by building new hospitals with modern medical equipment to bring its health delivery standards closer to those of other upper-middle-income countries. However, primary health care has not received the much needed investment and attention.

Among the positive developments during the implementation of the NHIP is that many NHIP beneficiaries have found it easier to afford health care. For example, (i) between 2008 and 2012 household out-of-pocket expenditures stabilized in nominal terms (from $144 to $163). Furthermore, these expenditures declined as a share of total health spending; they went from 51 percent in 2008 to 41 percent in 2012. (ii) The use of health services has risen throughout the population including the poor. (iii) Financial protection appears to be a positive trend. However, at this time, there is little data to explain how the NHIP has improved the financial protections of the poor. Additional household level data is necessary to determine that and to diagnose the constraints for accessing health care.

Gabon in Perspective

Over the years, Gabon's efforts have resulted in improved health outcomes of its population, but further efforts are required. Gabon is likely to achieve millennium development goal (MDG) target 1B on child malnutrition, if its efforts are maintained and amplified. Fertility remains significant, and communicable diseases remain the primary cause of morbidity and mortality. Although improvements are seen in human immunodeficiency virus/acquired immune deficiency syndrome (HIV/AIDS) incidence and tuberculosis incidence, malaria incidence remains high, and the country is not meeting MDG targets.

The country has made efforts to improve access to health services, and has been able to attain increased coverage in use of some areas, such as, antenatal care (95 percent, GDHS, 2013). There are also improvements in levels of institutional delivery of childbirth (90 percent, GDHS, 2013). However, quality of effective care remains low and thereby maternal mortality ratios are still high. While improvements are also seen in child health service use, such as immunization coverage, and improved use of some treatments (for example, ARI service use). However, knowledge and use of other effective treatments and services lag, such as limited knowledge and thereby use of oral rehydration therapy to prevent children to incurring dehydration from diarrhea. Child mortality reductions have slowed down given low attention given to effective services for prenatal and neonatal care. Generally, the quality of effective health care is poor all over the country, including in the public sector. This is especially true for the services availed by the poor and those living in rural areas. Gabon, however, is less likely to meet its MDG targets for health by 2015.

The book's findings show that while Gabon is an upper-middle-income country, its health outcomes are on a par with low to low-middle-income countries. For example, the life expectancy in Gabon is 63 years compared to upper-middle-income countries where the average life expectancy is 74 years (2011). Health outcomes, such as those for under 5 years child mortality (65 per 1,000 live births) and maternal mortality (230–316 per 100,000 live births), are closer to figures seen in other low-middle-income countries. However, the health of the Gabonese are considered to be worse off than other countries with similar incomes. Among the reasons cited for Gabon's poor health outcomes are: poverty, limited social protection programs, scant public resources for health, weak governance, and accountability mechanisms, and such systemic issues as inefficiencies in allocations within the health system.

Next Steps in Gabon's Path to Universal Health Coverage

Given that the country has moved toward a modality for NHIP, and aims to achieve universal health coverage, it is critical that priorities be set to address some of the next steps in Gabon's path to universal health coverage. Some key questions that need to be addressed are:

- Is the NHIP financially feasible—how are resources pooled, who pays, and what sources of financing need to be insured for its financial sustainability?
- Who benefits from the NHIP, and who is left out? How can the enrollment of those left out be insured to achieve universal health insurance coverage? What are the challenges and how can they be overcome?
- Is the benefits package offered under the NHIP financially affordable—who provides toward it, and who benefits from it?
- Are the entitlements under NHIP easily accessible and of acceptable standards?
- Is the purchasing mechanism under NHIP helping avoid moral hazard and supplier induced demand? Is the purchasing mechanism allowing improved performance?
- Are the administrative processes under NHIP leading to greater efficiency, equity, quality control standards, and cost containment?

What Could Work Better

Revenue Source

Increase public revenue from sources that are progressive: Gabon is looking at various options to increase revenue. General and earmarked taxes and levies finance the coverage of the poor under the GEF, and payroll taxes cover the non-poor formal sector workers. The financing for the NHIP in Gabon is regarded as a progressive tax. However, there is concern that the financing source for the GEF is not sustainable, and other options need to be considered.

Improve enrollment compliance and the collection of premiums: Enrollment remains incomplete. If it can be increased, it will automatically generate additional resources. The formal sector in Gabon is small and not fully enrolled, but the scope of contributions from the private sector remains uncertain. It is essential that the government quantify potential gaps in NHIP's budget.

Identify sources of financing for the coverage of informal sector workers under NHIP: The NHIP has been unable to create a mandatory or non-compensatory scheme for the non-poor who work in the informal sector. Many informal sector workers are in good health. They have the financial means, but they do not enroll in NHIP (adverse selection). Having them enroll in NHIP could diversify the risk pool even more. As a way to encourage their enrollment, incentives could be offered in the form of a more attractive term under a group premium. One solution could be to include this sub-group under public financing. A strategy would help with the assessment and steer the debate. An actuarial analysis of the benefits package would help identify the appropriate premium rate.

Type of Pooling Funds

Cross-subsidization: NHIP has three different schemes: (i) for the poor; (ii) for civil servants and the formal sector, and (iii) for the informal sector. The NHIP was established to ensure universal coverage. Coverage has been greatly and successfully expanded. Nevertheless, the schemes are fragmented and there are no clear plans for a pooling mechanism to allow cross-subsidization. With such institutional arrangements, it is unlikely that risk will be shared and effective cross-subsidization between the rich and poor and the healthy and the sick will occur. To ensure both progressivity and efficiency, it is highly recommended to (i) pool the risks for the general population and the poor, or (ii) set up formulas for cross-subsidization transfers between the different pools. The NHIP administrative costs are significant given that each of the schemes is run independently of the other.

Financial sustainability of health insurance: Furthermore, there is a lack of consistent cost estimates and no systematic actuarial study to ensure that each scheme is sustainable. As NHIP moves forward to establish new insurance schemes for population groups that are still not covered and it seeks to identify additional sources of funding for them, NHIP should first consider a comprehensive actuarial study of the current and proposed schemes, and consider an actuarially estimated premium.

NHIP reserve policy should be firmed up: Resources under NHIP's various schemes are not pooled and it is difficult to determine how much NHIP has in its reserves. Its reserves policy is not clear. Actuaries often recommend that reserves for a more mature health insurance program should have funds amounting to about 4–6 months of anticipated claims. A more thorough actuarial analysis would more accurately reveal what is in this reserve fund and it might offer some policy suggestions on the amounts that should be in reserve.

Population Covered

Eligibility of low-income groups: To be eligible for a health insurance subsidy, an adult must earn less than 80,000 XAF a month ($160), equal to the monthly minimum wage in Gabon. A national census was used to elaborate on the list of beneficiaries. Because means tests were difficult to administer, the current list reportedly contains errors and is likely to include wealthier quintiles. There is also discussion around changing eligibility criteria, including the possibility of an entire household, rather than individual incomes. Proposals to target government subsidies to the truly indigent are not only commendable but they also free up resources and reinforce equity and financial protections.

Mandatory coverage of the informal sector: Registration of informal sector workers is voluntary and there is little incentive for them to enroll. Lessons from other countries suggest that coverage of informal sector workers may be a challenge. More than 70 percent of Gabon's population comes from the informal sector. Often countries like Ghana and the Philippines have had registrations stalled because workers in the informal sector are hard to reach. Thailand on the other hand decided to subsidize the premiums of all informal sector workers under general taxes. There are pros and cons, subsidizing the informal sector could motivate the formal sector to increase informality (as seen in the Philippines); however, (partial or full) subsidies may help increase enrollment. Gabon will have to figure out how to offer an incentive for these workers to register. Critical questions that might help NHIP develop a policy are as follows: is there a demand, who will pay the premiums, will there be government subsidies, how much, and what will be the source of financing? NHIP plans to develop a strategy in 2015 and 2016 for covering informal sector workers.

Commodity Purchased

The benefit package: The benefit package under NHIP is comprehensive (outpatient, inpatient, and drugs), but curative in nature. It excludes those goods and services that are communicable, covered by the MOHPH or through external grant financing. It is imperative to ensure public health objectives are equally met and its coverage accelerated. Further, the benefit package under NHIP includes non-health coverage, such as a childbirth bonus and school spending for children up to 18 years of age. The NHIP premiums are not based on an actuarial estimate, and so it is not clear whether sufficient revenue is collected to cover the costs of care. However, an actuarial and financial sustainability analysis is planned for 2015 and 2016.

Purchasing Mechanism

Provider payment mechanism and the incentives for supplier-induced demand: NHIP uses a fee-for-service payment mechanism for services and for drugs at all types of facilities (health clinics to hospitals). This mechanism is known to result in supplier- induced demand. Service use has gone up; however, specifics are yet to be determined. This study was unable to collect information on how the pattern of services has changed. However, claims expenditures have increased significantly as a share of total NHIP spending and in per capita terms. Incentives arising from payment mechanisms are often distorted; for example, the high level of C-sections is clearly linked to the fact that providers receive a higher amount for them than normal deliveries. Other provider payment mechanism options, such as capitation at primary health care and case-mix payment at hospitals, can be considered.

Moral hazard: The fee-for-service provider payment system creates incentives for patients to use more services, while the copayments may result in reduction in moral hazard. The influence of copayments on the use of services by the poor need to be better understood. Does it create adverse effects?

Copayments and their effect on offering financial protection against the cost of illness: The country still does not offer financial protection. Much more is expected of a UMIC that aims to achieve universal health coverage. For one, over half of Gabon's population is not covered under NHIP. Second, all populations are subject to copayments, even if they are enrolled, and otherwise, they are expected to pay full user fees. Further, given poor quality of care at primary care, it is noteworthy that many of its beneficiaries are visiting hospitals for consultations instead of clinics. Travelling to urban centers to access hospitals adds to travel costs. Charges for similar consultation services at hospitals are higher than at clinics. Balance billing also exists in private health facilities. Although most of the poor do not use private health facilities, when they do, their health care costs could be even higher. Given the lack of household income-expenditure surveys, it is not clear what households spend on health. A benefit incidence analysis would provide an even better understanding of who benefits from government subsidies, but that analysis is not possible given limited information. However, a poverty survey at the household level is expected to be conducted in 2015 and could help with further analyses.

Expenditure Management

Except for cost sharing, revenue enhancements do little to improve spending efficiency; an increase in spending needs to be accompanied by improvements in the system's allocative and technical efficiency.

Timely release of resources: Releases from the treasury and tax departments are reportedly delayed. These delays affect the credibility of the funds, particularly for the poor and for civil servants. This subsequently effects the timely reimbursement from NHIP to the health providers.

Claims processing: NHIP has introduced electronic health systems (ehealth) to register beneficiaries. However, it has not yet introduced a comprehensive system that includes an electronic claims (eclaims) management system. Claims are processed manually. Providers indicate that reimbursements are often delayed. These delays could be a result of multiple factors: low releases from the treasury to NHIP, insufficient reserves, or manual claims processing. Because many providers rely heavily on off-budget for their operating costs, a delay in reimbursement can be very disruptive to a facility. Further assessment is required. That includes the development of an audit/fraud management cell to ensure the validation of claims.

Upgrading the quality of service and re-orienting budget subsidies: Inadequate quality of service creates unnecessary costs for the system (bypassing, follow-up visits, false prescribing patterns, overuse of high-cost services) and ultimately for patients' health outcomes. Gabon has made significant investment in responding to concerns of low quality care. It is necessary to elaborate on those efforts by focusing on primary and preventive care. Improving service coverage may require redistributing some of government health spending to lower levels of care (that is primary and preventive) so that those who are worse off may benefit more from government subsidies than is true today. Performance-based payments may also be an option for boosting the quality of service. Accreditation may be another; few non-public facilities in Gabon are accredited. This would improve efficiency in spending.

Note

1. Demand-side financing is a way in which the government can finance private consumption of certain goods. In contrast to supply-side financing, where public money goes directly to suppliers, consumers receive a certain amount of money for specific expenditures under demand-side financing. It emphasizes consumer choice; the consumer decides where public money will go. http://www.seor.nl/media/publications/economics-demand-side-financing.pdf.

CHAPTER 1

Background and Objectives

Economic Background

The Gabonese Republic is a vast geographical area with a small population. The country lies along the equator on the west coast of Africa. Its border is 2,551 kilometers long (1,585 miles) with a coastline of 885 kilometers (550 miles). Gabon is bound on the west by the Atlantic Ocean, on the north by Equatorial Guinea (350 kilometers/218 miles) and Cameroon (298 kilometers/185 miles), and to the east and south by the Republic of Congo (1,903 kilometers/1,183 miles). The country is divided into 9 provinces and 49 departments. There are 10 Regional Health Directorates (directions regionals de santé, DRS); the Estuaire Department is split into two DRS (Libreville-Owendo and Ouest).[1]

Over the past five years Gabon has enjoyed positive real economic growth. However, in future, its growth rates are expected to decline in current and constant prices. Gabon is an upper middle income country (UMIC) with a gross national income (GNI) of $10,040 per capita (2012). From 2005 to 2011, Gabon had a real gross domestic product (GDP) growth rate of 3 percent. Growth rates declined from 7.0 percent in 2011, to 4.2 percent in 2012 (World Development Indicators [WDI] database, 2013). World Bank forecasts suggest that GDP growth rates will decline to about 3.9 by 2016 (WDI 2013). Forty percent of its income comes from oil. However, oil revenues peaked in 2010 and the projection is they will decline in current and constant prices. From 2005 to 2010 fiscal revenue was stable at 30 percent of GDP. Nevertheless, revenue collection could have been improved (figure 1.1).

Gabon faces an increase in poverty. Between 1997 and 2005 poverty rates worsened. During that period, the percentage of those living below poverty went from 25 percent of the population to 33 percent (World Bank 2012b): in 2005 4 percent of the population lived on less than $1 a day and 19.6 percent lived on less than $2 per day (Wikipedia). The poor appear to be concentrated in the Northern and Southern regions of Gabon (54 percent and 44 percent, respectively). The Gini index for Gabon is 41.5 (2005).[2] Most of the country's resources are in the hands of the few; income inequality is widespread throughout

Figure 1.1 Gabon: Annual Growth Rate Based on GDP Per Capita, PPP

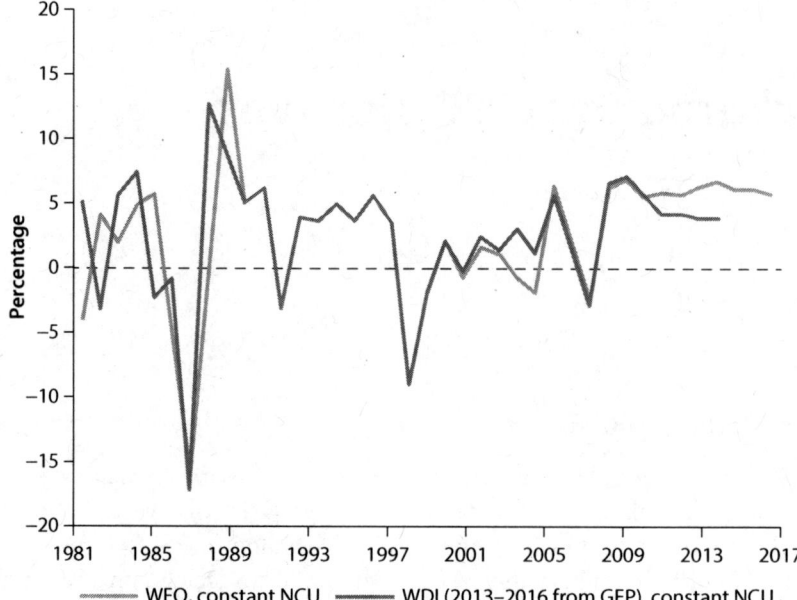

Source: International Monetary Fund (IMF) and World Bank.
Note: Projections are for 2013–17. GDP = gross domestic product; NCU = national currency unit;
PPP = purchasing power parity; WDI = World Development Indicators database; WEO = World
Economic Outlook database.

Table 1.1 Socioeconomic Indicators in African Countries, 2012

ranked by GNI

Country/region	GNI/capita[a]	GNI rank	HDI	HDI rank	Life expectancy	Mean schooling
Seychelles	22,615	37	0.806	46	73.8	9.4
Libya	13,765	56	0.769	64	75.0	7.3
Mauritius	13,300	63	0.737	80	73.5	7.2
Botswana	13,102	64	0.634	119	53.0	8.9
Gabon	12,521	66	0.683	106	63.1	7.5
South Africa	9,594	79	0.629	121	53.4	8.5
Algeria	7,418	97	0.713	93	73.4	7.6
Egypt, Arab Rep.	5,401	106	0.662	112	73.5	6.4
Morocco	4,394	117	0.591	130	72.4	4.4
Ghana	1,684	157	0.558	135	64.6	7.0

Source: Human Development Report 2013.
a. In 2005 purchasing power parity (PPP) $. GNI = gross national income; HDI = human development index.

Gabon. Social protection programs are limited. Many of those who were the near
poor slipped through the cracks when they experienced economic shocks or
catastrophic events. In the near future, the country could benefit from diagnosing
poverty, mitigating it, and scaling up its social protection programs (table 1.1).

Gabon continues to face significant inequity in its growth and living conditions. Eighty six percent of the population lives in urban areas; however, almost 40 percent of them live in underdeveloped areas/slums. Infrastructure is poorly developed, especially sanitation. Although more than 80 percent of the population has access to improved drinking water, less than 40 percent of the people have access to improved sanitation. Improving the population's access to clean water and sanitation has multiple benefits. These steps could also lead to an immediate improvement in health outcomes.

Population Dynamics and Demographic Changes

Gabon has a significant fertility rate; its youth will continue to have a demand for social services. The country has a population of 1.6 million and a population growth rate of 2.1 percent (1998–2008). The total fertility rate[3] is 4.2 (2012) (WDI 2013). The proportion of the population under age 15 is sizeable—37 percent. At these growth rates, the population will double by 2045. The dependency ratio[4] will decline from 78 percent in 2011 to 69 percent in 2025 (figure 1.2).

Figure 1.2 Demographic Profile, 2012–45

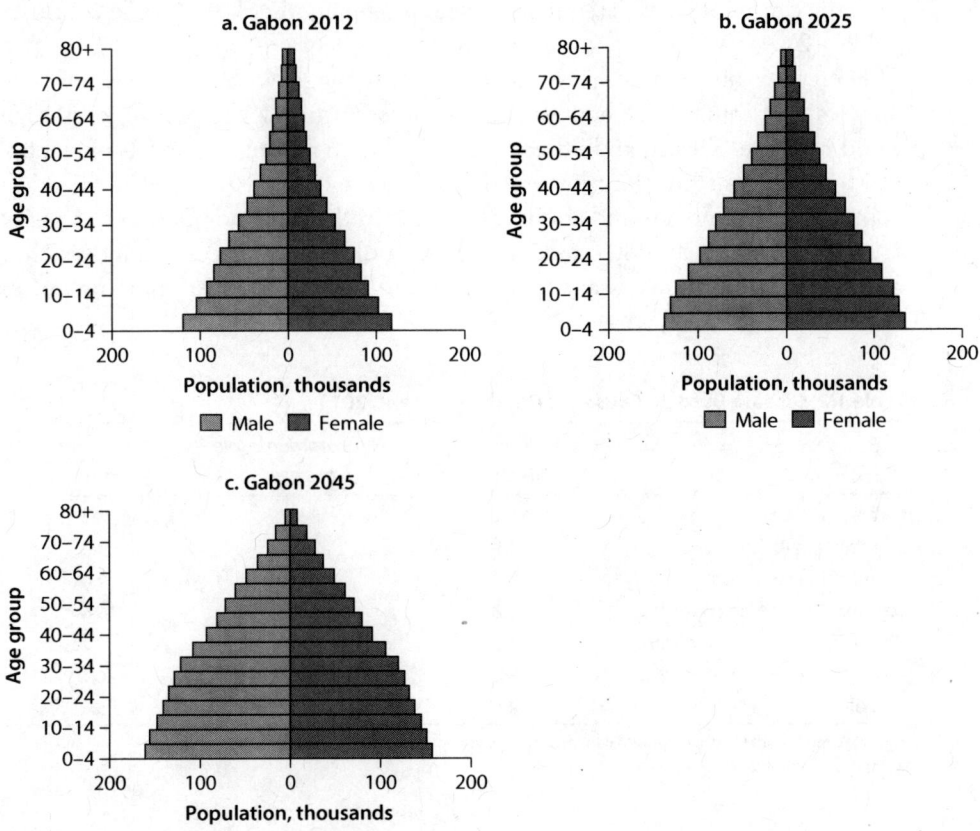

Source: World Bank's HealthStats database. http://datatopics.worldbank.org/hnp/.

Health Financing in the Republic of Gabon • http://dx.doi.org/10.1596/978-1-4648-0289-8

The human development index for Gabon stands at 106 out of 187 countries in 2012 (UNDP 2014). Literacy is universal (97 percent of those between 15 and 24 years). But the gross enrollment ratio is 72 percent for males and 68 percent for females (2005). Gabon also faces significant unemployment: 16 percent of men and 27 percent of women; the unemployment rate among youth under 30 years of age is 30 percent (2010). However, 70 percent of the labor force is expected to be in the informal sector. The country could benefit from realizing the demographic dividend.

Epidemiological Changes

Gabon is in the early stages of an epidemiological transition. Communicable diseases are prevalent and represent a significant proportion of the country's burden of disease. Malaria, for which cost-effective interventions exist, remains the most prevalent cause of morbidity among all age groups and the highest cause of death among children under 5 years. The prevalence of human immu-nodeficiency virus (HIV)[5] remains above the regional average (52 per 1,000 adults aged 15–49 years in 2010). Tuberculosis is double the regional average (676 per 100,000 population in 2010).[6] In Gabon the disease burden, as reflect-ed in the causes of death, is similar to what is seen in other low-income countries (table 1.2).

There is a need to address risk factors associated with noncommunicable diseases and injuries. Gabon shows an increase in risk factors, such as high blood pressure, obesity, and others. The population has relative levels of alcohol and tobacco consumption: since 2011, approximately 11 percent of the adult population are smokers and about 20 percent of the male population.[7] Stronger prevention and early detection programs would be more cost-effective; they could help avoid unnecessary treatments and lead to the cost containment of medical care.

Table 1.2 Disease Burden, Causes of Death in Percent, 2011

	Communicable diseases	Noncommunicable diseases	Injuries
Gabon	**55.7**	**36.7**	**7.7**
Sub-Saharan Africa	61.9	29.1	9.0
Low-income countries	54.3	36.4	9.4
Low-middle-income countries	33.8	55.8	10.4
Upper-middle-income countries	10.2	80.6	9.1
High-income countries	6.6	87.3	6.1
Global	24.5	66.4	9.1

Source: World Health Organization (WHO), http://www.who.int/healthinfo/global_burden_disease/estimates_regional/en/.

Health Service Infrastructure

Gabon has a comprehensive health service delivery network. The Gabonese health sector is composed of three main subsectors: a large public sector managed by the Ministry of Health and Public Hygiene (MOHPH) and other ministries, a "parapublic" sector made of a national health insurance program (NHIP), and a substantial private sector.

The public sector includes facilities operated and funded by the MOHPH as well as programs and facilities operated by other ministries, especially the Ministry of Defense. The Ministry of Defense operates a large Hopital d'Instruction des Armées Omar Bongo Ondimba (Hospital Instruction Armed Omar Bongo Ondimba; HIAOBO) hospital and garrison infirmaries for the armed forces. Other ministries that provide health care include the Ministry of Justice (which is responsible for health services to prisoners), the Ministry of Interior (Police Force), and the Ministry of Education (through university hospitals). MOHPH is taking over facilities previously owned by Social Security Scheme (Caisse Nationale de Securité Sociale, CNSS), namely two hospitals in Libreville and Port Gentil.

The MOHPH subsystem has three levels: central or strategic, regional or intermediate, and local (périphérique) or operational (figure 1.3). The structure, which resembles a pyramid, includes:

- Primary care level: Dispensaries and health posts (cases de santé) at the lowest, community level; health centers (Centres de Santé) in urban areas and Medical Centres (Centres Médicaux) as the reference facility for primary care at the departmental level;
- Secondary level: Regional Health Directorates (DRS) and coordinating structures (such as Epidemiology Bases, Sanitation and Maternal & Child

Figure 1.3 The Structure and Levels of the (Public) Health System in Gabon

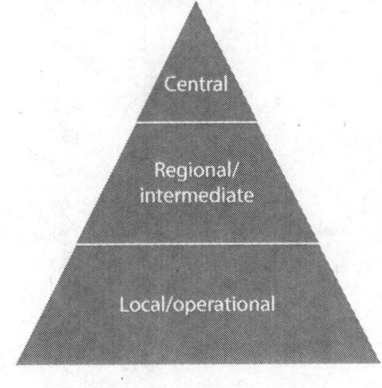

	Administration	Hospitals	PHC & Public Health
Central	Directions Centrales Instituts	CHU (Centres Hospitaliers Universitaires)	National/vertical programs
Regional/ intermediate	DRS—Directions Regionales de Santé	CHR—Centres Hospitaliers Régionaux -Hopitaux Régionaux	Bases d´Epidemiologie
Local/operational			ªCentres Médicaux Centres de Santé Dispensaires Cases de Santé

Source: World Bank on the basis of Ministry of Health documents.
Note: PHC = primary health care.
ªSome Medical Centers are being converted to Departmental Hospitals.

Health Financing in the Republic of Gabon • http://dx.doi.org/10.1596/978-1-4648-0289-8

Health Services) at the regional/provincial level oversees primary health care (PHC). Centres Hospitaliers Régionaux (Regional Hospitals; CHR) provide referral and hospital services;

- Tertiary/Central level: national/vertical programs and referral diagnostic services are managed centrally along with national administrative and technical offices and research institutes. Three tertiary-level hospitals are in Libreville.

The public sector provides the largest network of delivery services; however, parapublic sector facilities are critical for workers in the formal sector. CNSS used to run a "parapublic" system, which consisted of three hospitals: the Jeanne Ebory Maternity, which is currently closed; the Paul Igamba Hospital in Port Gentil; and a specialized hospital, in addition to a network of nine Medical Centers (Centres Médico-Sociaux) at the provincial level. CNSS facilities are being transferred to MOHPH. The private sector includes for-profit, not-for-profit and traditional providers, but the modern polyclinics, clinics, doctors' offices, laboratories, pharmacies, and drug distributors tend to be concentrated in larger cities. They include Albert Schweitzer Hospital, a large and well-known hospital in Lambarene, and Bongolo Evangelical Hospital in the Eastern Directions Regionales de Santé, smaller hospitals and mission health centers,[8] as well as facilities and services run by major public and private companies. Some of the oil companies include: COMILOG, TOTAL Gabon, COMUF, SOGARA (table 1.3).

Table 1.3 Health Facilities by Type and Ownership

Type of health facilities	Public	Parapublic: Caisse Nationale de la Securité Sociale (CNSS)	Private for-profit	Private not-for-profit	NGO/humani-tarian	Total
General hospitals	12	2		2[a]		16
Specialist hospitals	12	1				13
Clinics			19			19
Polyclinics		1	1			2
Medical centers	41	9				50
Mother and baby centers	51					51
Dispensaries	413			4[b]		417
Health posts	157					157
Health center	37				8	45
Private practice			79			79
Testing laboratories			4			4
Pharmacies			33			33
Total	**729**	**13**	**136**	**6**	**8**	**884**
Percentage	82%	1%	15%	1%	1%	100%

Source: National Health Strategy 2011–15.
Note: NGO = nongovernmental organization.
a. Hopitale Generale Schweitzer and Bongolo.
b. Catholic and Protestant missions.

Gabon has a well-developed health service delivery; however, primary health networks are not as widespread. The country has a huge network of health providers (both public and private). Health posts exist in some communities, but not all over the country. Health centers are widespread, but rural facilities experience challenges in retaining health staff and in accessing drugs. Many of them also do not have basic equipment, including adequate cold chain for vaccination. Given the huge communicable disease burden in the country, public health outreach programs appear deficient too.

The country offers many hospital-beds, mostly concentrated in urban centers. Hospital-bed ratios (6.3 hospital beds per 1,000 population in 2010)[9] are significantly higher than necessary in a country with the disease burden it has. Furthermore, although bed occupancy rates at tertiary hospitals are reasonable, they are low at regional hospitals (averaging about 40 percent) (table 1.4 and figure 1.4).

Table 1.4 Hospital Bed Ratios Per 1,000 Population

	Hospital beds per 1,000 population (2006–11)
Gabon	**6.3**
Upper-middle-income country	3.5
High-income country	4.3
Euro area	5.7

Source: WDI 2013, http://wdi.worldbank.org/table/2.15.

Figure 1.4 Hospital Bed Ratios Compared to Other Countries of Similar Income and Health Spending

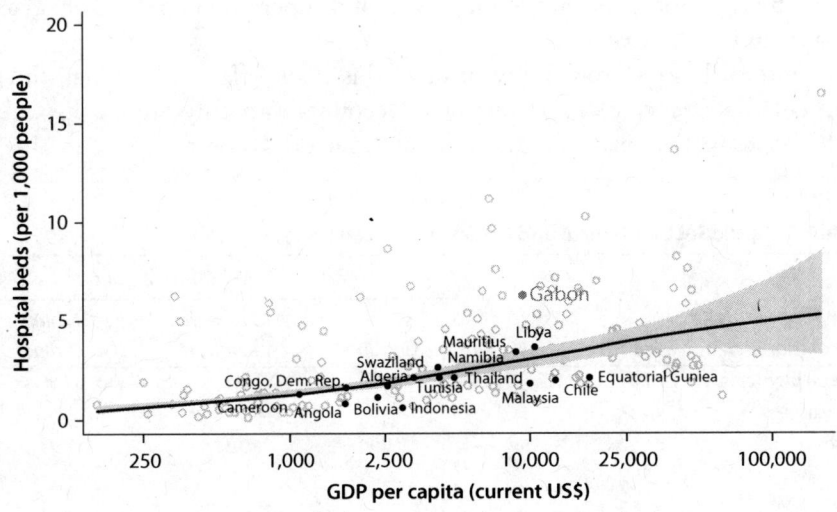

Health Service Providers

Health staffing in Gabon is promising. Gabon's statistics on physician are within range of the World Health Organization and Joint Learning Network's (WHO-JLN) recommendations (Gabon has 0.3 physicians per 1,000 population). However, they are lower than countries with similar incomes and health spending. The country also surpasses WHO's recommendations for nurse-midwife ratios (Gabon's is 5 per 1,000 population) (table 1.5 and figure 1.5).

Health personnel distribution is skewed toward larger cities and urban areas. Staffing norms, although they exist, are not always applied. In 2005, 48 percent of health personnel were concentrated in Libreville-Owendo. All other health regions had between 9 percent and 3 percent of the total. Based on available data for 2013, 69 percent of university-level staff is concentrated in two regions: Libreville-Owendo and the Centre-Sud (capital: Mouila). The ratio per 100 population varies between 90 and 0 based on the department. Three health regions have a density higher than the national average of 1.5 (Libreville-Owendo, Ouest and Centre-Sud). Five regions have less than 20 percent of the national average (Sud-Est, Centre, Sud, Est, Nord). Certainly a more equitable distribution of staffing based on need would lead to improved efficiency and effectiveness (figure 1.6 and box 1.1).

Staff accountability mechanisms are weak. Public providers serve in both public and private facilities with few controls. Further, based on a general audit of civil servants, accountability mechanisms are weak and staff absenteeism appears to be rampant; that is especially true outside the major cities.[10] There is little information on staff knowledge, attitudes, and practices. However, training and supportive supervision seems weak. Incentives must be reviewed to ensure that they motivate staff and improve their performance. A performance orientation with appropriate incentives for service and supervision could likely change behavior in the positive direction.

In spite of limited availability of data, this book offers substantial, though fragmented, evidence of a serious lack of accountability throughout the Gabon health system. For example, the central level does not feel accountable to

Table 1.5 Public Sector Medical and Paramedical Staff by Type

			Cadre ratio to 1,000 population		
Type of cadre	Public sector	%	Gabon	WHO low-end benchmark	WHO-JLN high-end benchmark
General physician	209	8	0.32	0.1	0.55
Specialists	283				
Nurses	5,112	92	3.39	0.3	1.9
Midwives	559				
Total	6,163				

Source: Ministry of Health Carte Sanitaire 2008.
Note: WHO = World Health Organization; WHO-JLN = World Health Organization and Joint Learning Network.

Figure 1.5 Human Resource Population Ratio as Compared to Other Countries of Similar Income and Health Spending

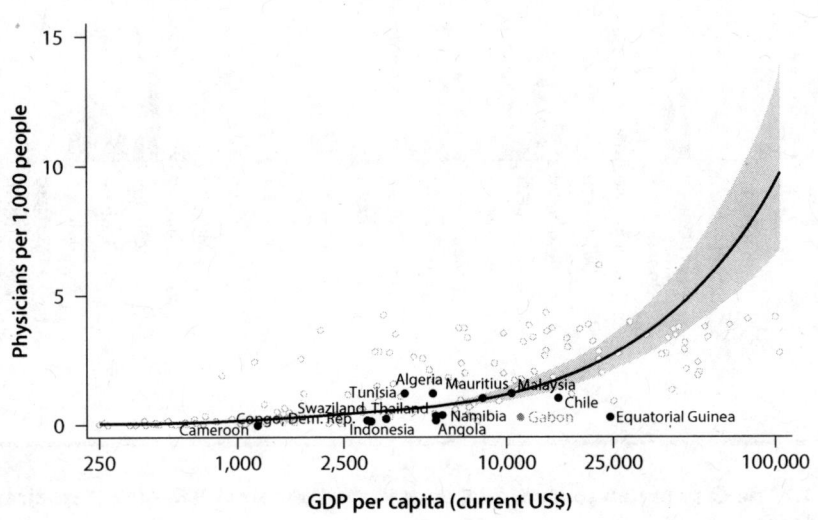

a. Physician ratio

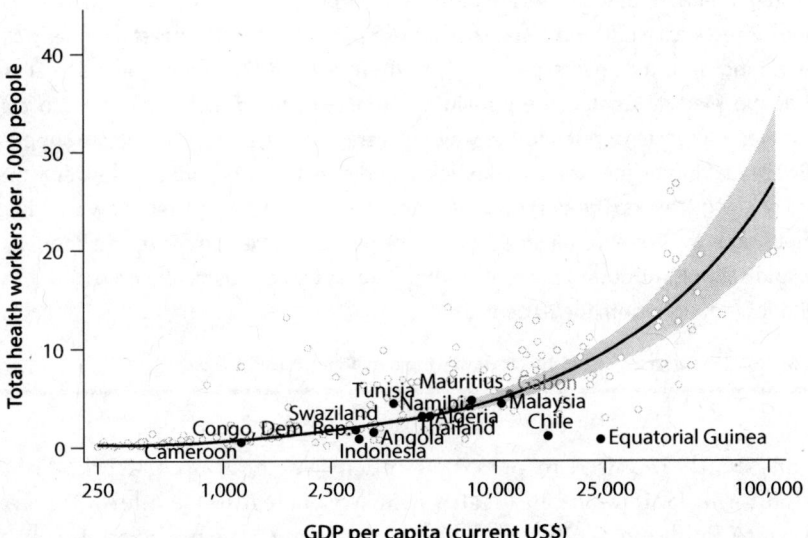

b. Health workers ratio

healthcare facilities in ensuring them with a predictable budget and resources. Moreover, a transparent regulatory and policy framework is lacking. The central level collects little, if any, information on the (poor) conditions in which most facilities, especially at the primary level, operate. On the other hand, facility managers and staff are paid base salaries plus a number of allowances and bonuses—without any transparent link to performance. Managers and staff are

Figure 1.6 Density of University-Level Staff at Primary Health Care Facilities Per 100 Population, 2012

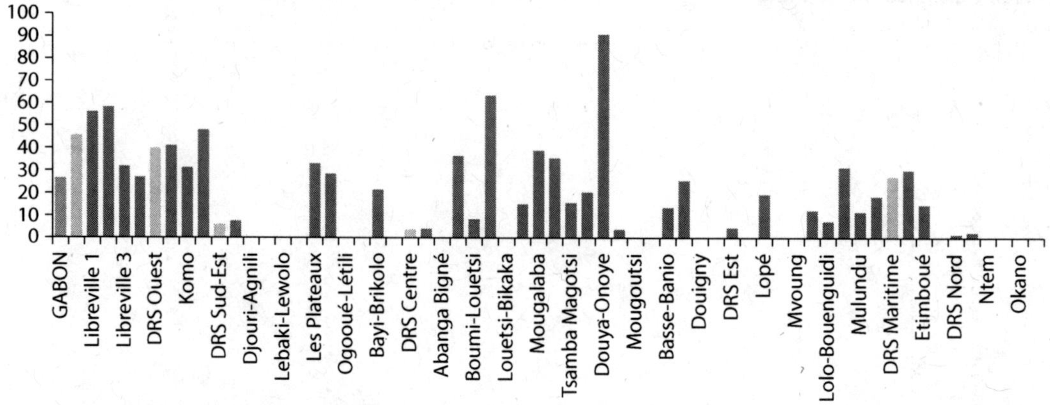

Source: Ministry of Health/COSP.

Box 1.1 The Case of Kango Medical Center in the West Health Region (Estuaire Province)

Staffing issues: The Health Department, which covers a population of 20,000 and 10 facilities, has 43 staff members, of which 30 are permanent (1 physician, 1 nurse, 2 midwives, 23 nursing aides, 2 technical staff, and 1 statistician). Nonpermanent staff consists of nearly all support (cleaning, security, drivers, secretary). Thirty-three staff (77 percent of the total) are located at the Medical Center; the remaining 10 are scattered across nine health centers, dispensaries and posts, or put another way, an average of 1.1 staff per facility. To supplement insufficient staffing at the lower facility level, additional staff is paid by the Departmental Council or Town Mayors. The department is not able to attract and retain new staff because little housing is available in the area. Lower facilities also have poor water, inadequate electricity, and schools. About 40 percent of the Medical Center has been converted into staff dormitories (enough room for 20 beds).

Source: World Bank's personal visit and interviews with health staff and review of records.

---

not consistently required to perform—much less show up at work. Although the Monitoring Unit for Public Health, Ministry of Health (Cellule d'Observation de la Santé Publique, COSP), collects general data, it is not geared or used to measure facilities' performance. Fragmentation of authority between the MOHPH and NHIP (under the Ministry of Economy) exacerbates the lack of accountability; no one seems to be "in charge" of running the system.

Realizing these constraints, the government has taken steps to improve the efficiency and effectiveness of public sector facilities. For instance, several public hospitals have had their management partially outsourced to a private company to improve facility management. But, as a result, hospital management has to comply with inefficient and rigid procurement regulations (for example for drugs) that in fact have greatly reduced its ability to make genuine improvements.

There is also evidence of other supply-side shortages, such as medical equipment, reagents and drugs. Drug procurement is centralized; however, distribution networks are poor and budgets for drugs are limited, factors that often constrain timely distribution of drugs. Over time, off-budget sources of financing are filling the gaps in financing drug supplies. Also, certain staffing policies, such as access to pharmacists, have adversely affected access to drugs at lower level facilities.

Health Policy and Strategy

To improve the health and welfare of its population, the country aims to achieve universal health coverage as well as enhance the quality of care. The MOHPH has prepared a National Health Development Plan 2011–15 (PNDS 2011), that has identified seven strategic activities to unfold in annual operational plans:

- Provide universal health care coverage
- Develop quality and accessible care
- Strengthen the governance of the health system and MOHPH leadership
- Make available quality essential drugs and devices, vaccines, blood products, and diagnostic services
- Develop human resources
- Develop sustainable mechanisms for health financing and social protection
- Set up an effective national health information system (including health surveillance), and develop health research.

Further, the country has also prioritized investment under the Growth and Poverty Reduction Strategy Paper (GPRSP 2006–08 in World Bank [2012]). The health sector is among its priorities. Fifteen objectives were grouped into four general objectives in the GPRSP to be covered over three years (2007–09): (i) improving maternal and child health, (ii) strengthening the fight against major diseases, (iii) improving the availability of basic services and the supply and quality of health services to vulnerable populations, and, (iv) improving the organization, functioning and management of the national health system (World Bank 2012b).

The main legal and regulatory documents governing the health sector include the following:

- Decree 0001/95, which defines the national health policy
- The law on the general status of public service (2005) and Decree 00867/MSPP/1981, particularly public servants in social sectors
- Decree 00646/MSPP/1971 on the organization and operation of health facilities

- Decree 1158/MSPP/1997 determining the structure and responsibilities of the MOHPH
- The contract between the government and the VAMED[11] consortium on the comanagement of public hospitals.

Financial management in the public health sector is governed by the following regulations:

- Decree 00384/MSPP/1968, which regulates private practice and its remuneration by health professionals
- Decree 00848/DSP-BA/1969, which established the Common Hospital Fund
- Decree 1334/MSPP/1980 on hospitalization fees
- Decree 00317/MSPP/1995 regulating medical internships
- Decree 314/MSPP/1969 regulating pricing of health services in the private sector
- Decree 00918/MSPP/1969 defining the incentives structure for health sector civil servants
- Regulation 09/MSPP/CAB1/1985 on cost recovery.

Historical Perspective on the Evolution of Health Financing Reform

A law (law 3/91 dating back to March 26, 1991) committed to providing free health care services. As a result, the government subsidized health care at public facilities for many population sub-groups. Although economic growth in the 1980s was positive, the rates slowed in the 1990s. During periods of recession between 1999 and 2002, the government considered income generation opportunities. As a consequence, in 1995, user fees or copayments went into effect for acute care at hospitals, but these fees did not allow the system to recover from recurrent deficits and deficiencies (Inoua and Musango 2013; Musanga and Inoua 2010).

From 2003 to 2004, as economic growth improved, resources for health also increased, including the public sector. In 2007, the former President of Gabon, Omar Bongo, supported a reform to establish an NHIP under the Caisse Nationale d'Assurance Maladie et de Garantie Sociale (National Health Insurance and Social Security; CNAMGS). The law was ratified in 2007 (Decret 00510/2008). A major outcome: funding patterns of the Gabonese health system were reorganized under the NHIP.

Book Objectives

Since 2007, Gabon has embarked on an NHIP for universal health insurance coverage. With the introduction of the NHIP, the country has redirected its resources toward demand-side financing.[12] Because of this, certain segments have called for additional resources for the sector. As a result, the country is grappling with the following: (i) how are resources being spent, (ii) is there room for a more efficient allocation of existing resources or (iii) is there an immediate need to mobilize additional resources to meet the country's goals of universal health coverage. This book attempts to diagnose the situation and provide more information to enlighten this debate.

This is a product of a World Bank's Economic Sector Work study that diagnosed health financing in Gabon. The book includes various elements: (i) a health systems overview, (ii) health financing system overview, (iii) the national health insurance program Caisse Nationale de Securité Sociale (CNAMGS), (iv) fiscal space analysis relative to health, and (v) options for reform. A global benchmarking exercise also examined health outcomes and health spending. For this book the authors benefited from the country's institutional and budget data and from various secondary data, such as the Demographic Health Survey (GDHS 2013), newly estimated figures from the National Health Accounts (NHA database, 2013),[13] reports compiled and estimated by various other international development agencies, including the International Monetary Fund (IMF), the World Bank, World Development Indicators (WDI), the World Health Organization (WHO), and others. While on mission in July 2013, interviews were also conducted with staff at the MOHPH, the Ministry of Budget, the Ministry of Economy, CNAMGS, and some selected public sector health facilities. Some of the shortcoming of this study include: (i) limited in-depth data on health services, its use and its quality; (ii) limited information on households and their choice of services used and their health spending patterns. For example, the last household survey was conducted in 2005 before the introduction of the NHIP. The book could also have benefited from a benefit incidence analysis to assess who among the population sub-groups benefited from government subsidies.

The book has six chapters including this one. Chapter 2 provides an overview of the country's health status and service use patterns. Chapter 3 provides an overview of health financing systems and outputs. Chapter 4 provides an overview of the CNAMGS. Chapter 5 provides fiscal space analysis for health. Finally, Chapter 6 provides the reform issues and policy options in health financing. The key findings of this book are highlighted in the executive summary.

Notes

1. http://en.wikipedia.org/wiki/Gabon.
2. The Gini index measures the extent to which the distribution of income or consumption expenditures among individuals or households within an economy deviates from a perfectly equal distribution. A Lorenz curve plots the cumulative percentages of total income received against the cumulative number of recipients, starting with the poorest individual or household. The Gini index measures the area between the Lorenz curve and a hypothetical line of absolute equality, expressed as a percentage of the maximum area under the line. Thus a Gini index of 0 represents perfect equality, while an index of 100 implies perfect inequality. World Bank.

3. The total fertility rate is the number of children that are expected to be born to women of child-bearing age. A rate of about 2.1 will produce a stable population. If it is less than this, the population will decline unless the shortfall is made up by immigration.

4. The formula is youth under 14 years of age as a proportion of the population in the working-age group (15–64 years).

5. Human immunodeficiency virus.

6. WHO. May 2012. Gabon: Health Profile.

7. WHO. Country Profile. Tobacco Free Initiative.

8. All these hospitals receive substantial subsidies from the government.

9. World Development Indicators, 2013. http://data.worldbank.org/indicator/SH.MED. BEDS.ZS.

10. Ageneral audit of civil servants showed "These efforts to improve economic governance also included an audit of the number of government employees which revealed close to 7,000 ghost workers, that is, 10 percent of the total number of civil servants whose removal from the payroll should result in a significant reduction in the public wage bill." World Bank. 2012. Gabon Public Expenditure Review.

11. http://www.vamed.com/index.php?id=223&L=7.

12. Demand-side financing enables a government to finance private consumption of certain goods. In contrast to supply-side financing, where public money goes directly to suppliers, consumers receive a certain amount of money for specific expenditures under demand-side financing. The consumer decides where public money will go. http://www.seor.nl/media/publications/economics-demand-side-financing.pdf.

13. http://apps.who.int/nha/database/Key_Indicators_by_Country/Index/en? COUNTRYKEY=84537.

CHAPTER 2

Health Outcomes, and Use of Health Services

Introduction

This chapter provides background on progress the country has made in health outcomes. It offers a perspective on where Gabon stands on this subject when compared to other countries of similar income and health spending. It also provides insight on the extent to which the population has access to health services and what are some of its challenges.

Key Findings

- It is highly likely Gabon will achieve its MDG target 1B on child malnutrition if its efforts are maintained and amplified.
- Gabon is however less likely to meet its millennium development goal (MDG) targets for maternal and child health by 2015.
- Based on countries of similar income and health spending, it is not meeting its health outcome levels.
- Communicable diseases remain the primary cause of morbidity and mortality. Although, improvements are seen in human immunodeficiency virus/acquired immune deficiency syndrome (HIV/AIDS) incidence and Tuberculosis incidence, malaria incidence remains high, and the country is not meeting MDG targets.
- The country has made efforts to improve access to health services, and has been able to attain universal coverage in use of some maternal health outputs, such as antenatal care. There are improvements in levels of institutional delivery. However, quality of care remains low and thereby maternal mortality ratios are still high.
- While improvements are also seen in child health service use, such as immunization coverage, and improved use of acute respiratory infection (ARI) treatments, however, knowledge of use of others remain behind. Child

mortality reductions have slowed down given low attention given to prenatal and neonatal care.

- Further, health services continue to face challenges. The country experiences economic and geographical inequities in the use of health services.
- Most of the population relies on public facilities for health care, regardless of their economic status.
- Generally, the quality of health care is poor all over the country, including in the public sector. This is especially true for the poor and those living in rural areas.
- Gabon has a well-developed health service delivery system; however, its primary health network is not widespread.
- Gabon has more hospital beds than it needs for a country with its burden of disease profile.
- Although the numbers of medical and paramedical personnel are reasonable, they are not distributed equitably across the country. Furthermore their performance could be enhanced.
- Health systems and staff accountability mechanisms are limited.

Health Outcomes

Based on countries of similar income and health spending, Gabon is not meeting the health outcome it established. Gabon shows a relatively low life expectancy at birth of 63 years (60 years for males, and 64 years for females in 2011) (WDI 2013). Similarly, the under-5 mortality rate (U5MR) is below that of countries of similar incomes and health spending (rate of 65 per 1,000 live births in 2012, Gabon Demographic Health Survey [GDHS]). The maternal mortality ratio (MMR), which is also significant, ranges between 230 (WHO, et. al., 2010b) and 316 (GDHS 2013) per 100,000 live births[1] (figure 2.1).

Figure 2.1 Health Outcomes Relative to Countries of Similar Income

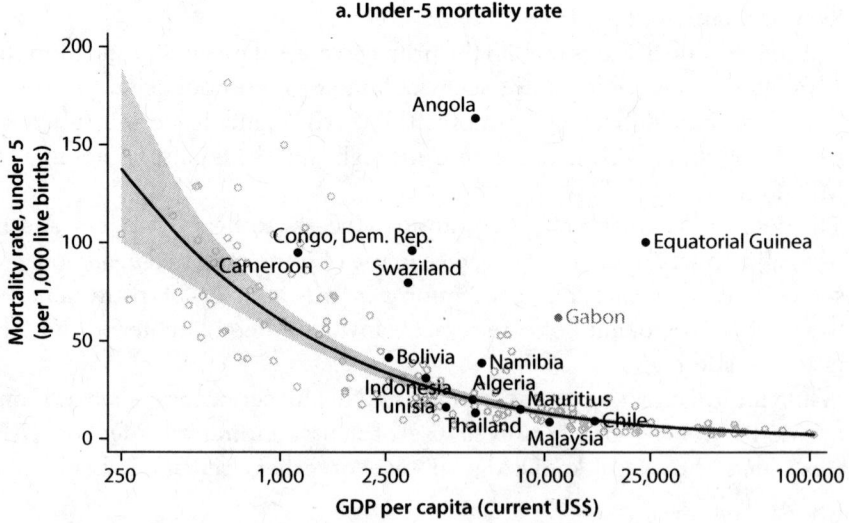

a. Under-5 mortality rate

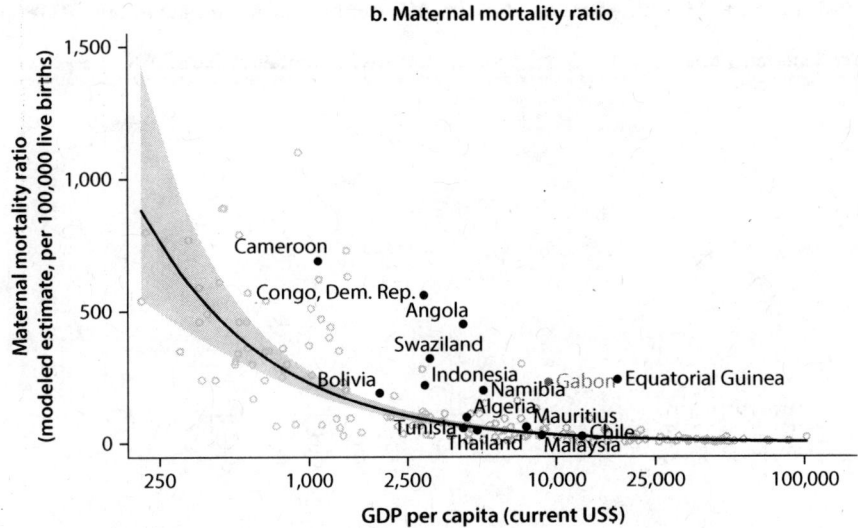

b. Maternal mortality ratio

Source: World Development Indicators, WHO, updated in Apr 2014
Note: x–axix log scale
Gray area indicated 95% confidence interval for the fitted line

By 2015 Gabon is less likely to meet its millennium development goal (MDG) targets for health. Not only is Gabon not meeting the MDG targets for under-5 mortality and maternal mortality, in some cases, these rates have increased or shown insignificant declines. Bringing the country on target will require much more effort. This is a major concern for the country (figure 2.2).

Maternal mortality in Gabon has shown insufficient progress in reduction in the past decade. The reasons for the poor health outcomes need urgent attention. Women are dying in childbirth; hemorrhages and hypertension are among the chief causes of their mortality. This problem can be addressed with institutional deliveries and with good emergency referral networks. In 2010, about 25 percent of maternal deaths in Gabon were an indirect result of AIDS-related conditions.[2] The prevalence of contraceptives remains at 31 percent; in 2012 the unmet need for contraceptives was 26 percent. While the use of contraceptives is low, the unmet need for contraceptives is significant; it is also higher among lower income groups. Addressing the unmet need for contraception would also help reduce maternal deaths (figure 2.3).

Recent trends in health outcome reductions are not promising. Although the rates for under-5 mortality rate (U5MR) and infant mortality rate (IMR) in Gabon have declined since 1992–96 to date, results for the recent past decade have not been promising. Mortality rates have nearly stagnated at approximately 65 for U5MR and 43 for IMR (GDHS 2013). The Northern region continues to be among the worst performers; the Eastern region continues to be among the best performers. Understanding the reasons behind this situation requires further study so that the obstacles to improving child health outcomes can be removed. In tandem with that, the inequity in health outcomes within

Figure 2.2 Trend in Under-5 Mortality Rate and Maternal Mortality Ratio as Compared to MDG Targets

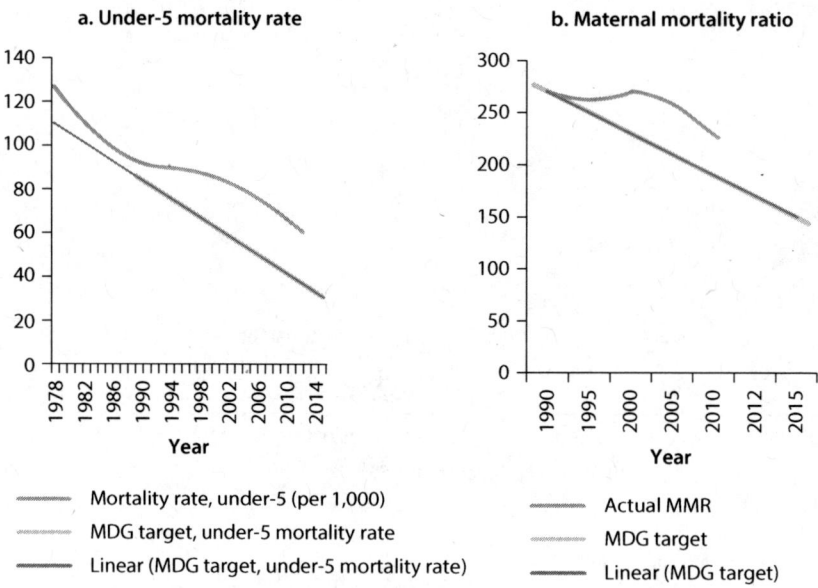

Source: World Health Organization (WHO), under-5 mortality rate (U5MR), Infant Mortality Rate (IMR): http://www.childinfo. org/mortality_igme.html; Maternal mortality ratio (MMR): http://www.who.int/reproductivehealth/publications/monitoring/ 9789241503631/en/.
Note: MDG = millennium development goal.

Figure 2.3 The Causes of Maternal Deaths by Percent

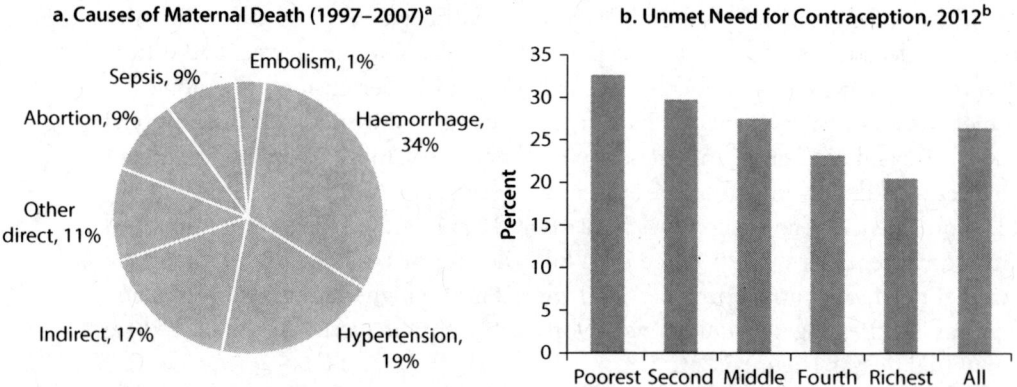

Sources: Panel a: WHO. March 2012. Gabon Country Profile: Maternal, Newborn and Child Survival. http://www.childinfo.org/files/ maternal/DI%20Profile%20-%20Gabon.pdf; panel b: GDHS 2013.

the country—geographically and economically—should also be addressed and remedied (figure 2.4).

Evidence suggests that child mortality (under 5 years of age) has been slow in its decline. At least 40 percent of child deaths occur in the first month of life (neonatal). This situation stems from the care that pregnant women receive and the care babies receive at birth and during the first month of life.

Figure 2.4 Trends in Under-5 Mortality and Infant Mortality Rates

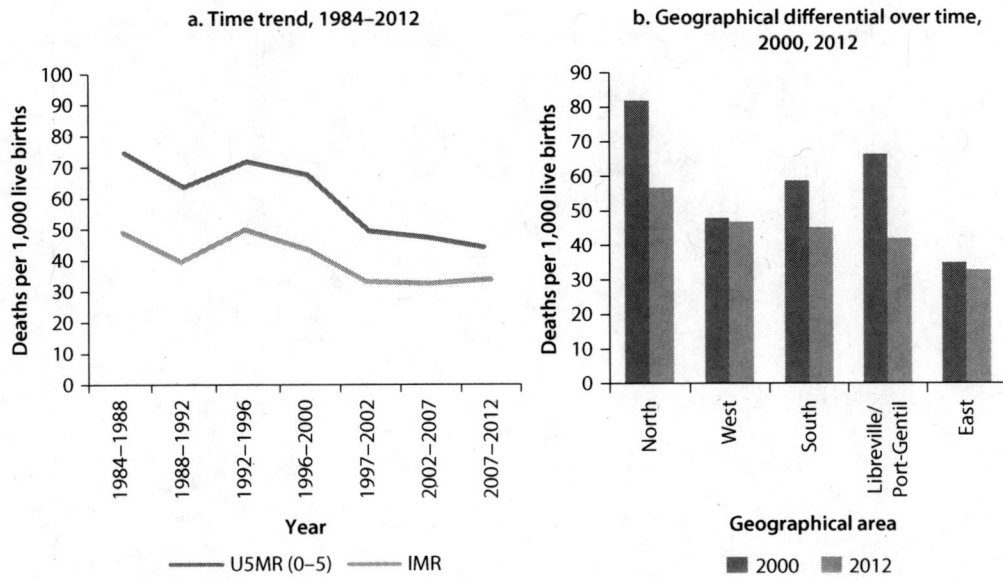

a. Time trend, 1984–2012

b. Geographical differential over time, 2000, 2012

Source: GDHS 2001, 2013.
Note: MMR = Maternal mortality ratio; U5MR = under-5 mortality rate.

Furthermore, for a reduction in child mortality to occur, much less accelerate, attention must be paid to preventing illness and improving the nutrition and immunity of infants. That means encouraging breastfeeding early in their lives, receiving vaccinations in a timely fashion, and protecting against childhood illnesses, such as diarrhea, upper respiratory infections, and malaria. These interventions are within reach and affordable. However, household knowledge, namely when to seek treatment, needs to be enhanced; likewise, the quality of care rendered by providers. Children from rural areas and from poorer households are even more disadvantaged.

Gabon is going through a nutritional transition. In 2012, about 6.5 percent of children (under 5 years) were malnourished (weight for age) and about 7.7 percent were overweight. Boys are more likely to be malnourished and overweight. Overall that same year, 17.5 percent children were considered to be stunted (height for age) and 3.4 percent were considered to be wasted.[3] Breastfeeding practices are not prevalent: only 32 percent of infants were breastfed within the first hour of birth and just 6 percent of infants were fully breastfed until 6 months of age. The MDG goal for 2015 is for malnourished children to represent no more than 5 percent of the population. It is highly likely Gabon will achieve its MDG target 1B if its efforts are maintained and amplified (MDG Report 2013).

Communicable diseases remain the primary cause of morbidity and mortality. Gabon shows a pattern of disease burden faced by low income countries. The greatest contribution to loss of life is communicable diseases (56 percent) followed by noncommunicable diseases (37 percent) and injuries (8 percent) (WHO 2011)[4] (figure 2.5).

Figure 2.5 Causes of Mortality, in Percent, 2010

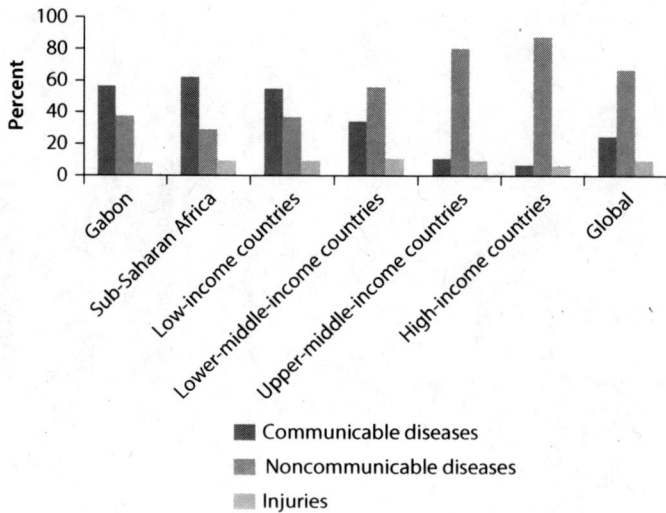

Source: WHO 2011.

- Cost-effective interventions for malaria exist. And yet, this disease remains the most prevalent cause of morbidity among all age groups and the highest cause of death among children under 5 years of age. Fever (resulting in acute respiratory infections or malaria) is quite prevalent among children. However, the percent of households reporting under-5 children with fever declined in the past decade, possibly as a result of improved living conditions. Fifty-one percent of children were sleeping under bednets in 2012.
- Between 2001 and 2011, Gabon was able to reduce the rate of new HIV infections by 54 percent. This is a remarkable achievement. Coverage of antiretroviral therapy among adults also increased from 23 percent in 2006 to 67 percent. But in 2012 coverage among children remained low at 24 percent.[5] However, it is highly likely for young boys (under the age of 15 years) to have intercourse. Meanwhile, among adult men (15–49 years) it is highly likely for them to have multiple partners. In 2012 the prevalence of HIV among adults 15–49 years was 4 percent.[6]
- Tuberculosis (TB) rate has declined over time (from 586 in 2002 to 428 per 100,000 population in 2012) (WDI 2013). This is a result of the success of the TB program. The TB detection rate under directly observed treatment, short-course (DOTS)[7] improved (from 28 percent in 2002 to 71 percent in 2012). However, under DOTS, there was little change noted in TB detection treatment which went from 47 percent in 2002 to 51 percent in 2011.
- Neglected Tropical Diseases (NTD) remains a significant public health challenge in Gabon. Several important NTDs are contributing to the burden of disease among the poor in forest and urban populations (including onchocerciasis, elephantiasis, schistosomiasis and geohelminthiasis).
- Among noncommunicable disease, the prevalence of diabetes increased in 2012 to about 10 percent of adults (ages 20–79 years).

Figure 2.6 Main Causes of Morbidity and Mortality, for All Ages, in Percent, 2005

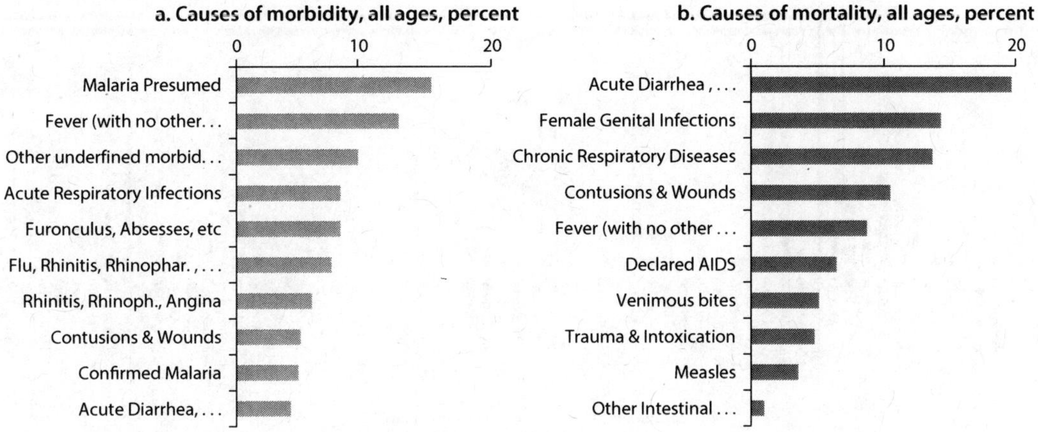

Source: Direction Générale de la Statistique et des Études Economiques (DGS) *Annuaire Statistique,* 2009.

The country is in its early stages of epidemiological transition, and will continue to have demands on it to control and prevent communicable diseases and to stem an increase in noncommunicable diseases. Primary health care should address both of these health concerns (figure 2.6).

Health Service Use

Overall, the use of health services has gone up over the years; however, wide variations exist across regions and by facilities. Access to and utilization of health services is very unequal across regions and departments. Large variations are found in the rates of medical consultations/100 population and hospital admissions/1,000 population, with ratios up to 1:100 across health regions and across departments within regions (figure 2.7 and table 2.1).

Maternal Health

There has been good use of services for maternal care. In the past decade prenatal care has remained consistently above 90 percent. Institutional delivery appears to be a generally accepted practice (at 90 percent in 2012). However, other aspects of health care are not as evident: the use of postnatal care is low. Family planning is also low.

There is economic and geographical inequity in the use of health services. Due to demand and supply-side constraints, inequity exists in the use of health services. Economic disparities are evident: 67 percent of the lowest consumption quintile used skilled birth attendants compared to 97 percent of the high consumption quintile who did so. Rural-urban differentials are also common: more than 90 percent of urban women delivered in a health facility compared to 70 percent of rural women who did so (GDHS 2013). Regional differentials are also

Figure 2.7 Health Service Utilization by Health Regions and Departments, 2012

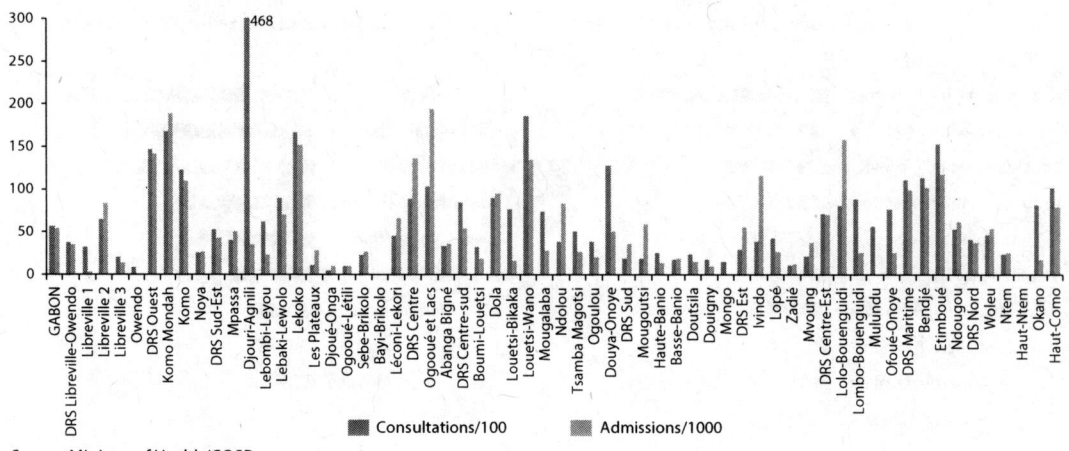

Source: Ministry of Health/COSP.
Note: DRS = Regional health directorates.

evident with the region of *Ogooué-Ivindo* being among the most notable on the low end. Institutional information systems are weak. Where data exists, it is scant and highlights the public sector only. The country continues to rely on population-based surveys to validate data on service coverage (figure 2.8).

Women are unable to access health facilities primarily due to distance and the cost of care. Overall, distance and treatment costs are cited as barriers to accessing health care. Among rural and urban women, distance to services is the primary reason they have chosen not to deliver at health facilities. The cost of treatment was also cited as contributing to their decision; a factor that was particularly true of rural women (GDHS 2013). Poorer women were disproportionately affected (figure 2.9).

Health services performance continues to face challenges, especially in the provision of basic health care and referrals. Although 95 percent of pregnant women receive antenatal care and a significant proportion of them give birth in health facilities, maternal mortality remains high (GDHS 2013). Meanwhile, the quality of care remains weak. Few women at prenatal care clinics received all the necessary (seven exams) care they needed from providers. Although the quality of care was poor throughout the country, the poor were disproportionately affected (figure 2.10).

Child Health

While the use of health services has gone up over the years, some services, such as preventive care, are still not as widely used. For example, few children are sleeping under bednets (51 percent), despite evidence that their use prevents malaria. Immunization is another example where gaps in coverage exist. Although measles vaccination went up from 55 percent in 2000 to 74 percent in 2011, there still is room for improvement (GDHS 2013). The lack of basic knowledge by consumers on the care and treatment of diarrhea is another case

Table 2.1 Health Related Indicators for Gabon

Indicators	2000 (GDHS 2001)	2012 (GDHS 2013)
Infant mortality rate, per 1,000 live births	57	43
Under-5 mortality rate, per 1,000 births	84	65
Maternal mortality ratio, per 100,000 live births	519 (GDHS 2001);	316 (GDHS 2013)
	420 (WHO 2000)	230 (WHO 2010);
		520 (PNDS 2010)
Contraceptive use	33% (12% modern)	31% (19% modern)
Prenatal care visits (%)	94%	95%
Postnatal care visits (%)		66%
Institutional deliveries (%)	85%	90%
		Urban 94%; rural 70%
Children (12–23) with full immunization coverage (%)	17%	32%
	(measles = 55%)	(measles = 74%)
Children U5 with ARI symptoms	13%	8%
Children U5 with malaria (fever)	29%	24%
Children U5 with diarrhea	16%	16%
Children U5 with ARI receiving treatment (%)	48%	68%
	(urban 52%, rural 34%)	(urban 71%, rural 52%)
Children U5 with diarrhea receiving ORT (%)	33%	37%
Children U5 with fever seeking treatment (%)	62%	67%
Children U5 with fever taking antimalarials (%)	—	26%
Children U5 sleeping under a mosquito net (%)	—	51%

Source: Gabon Statistical Service. Gabon Demographic Health Survey 2001, 2013, WHO, UNICEF, UNFPA and the World Bank estimates. *Trends in maternal mortality: 1990 to 2010.*
Note: ARI = acute respiratory infection; GDHS = Gabon Demographic Health Survey; ORT = oral rehydration therapy; PNDS = National Health Development Plan; U5 = under-five; WHO = World Health Organization; — = not available.

Figure 2.8 Child Birth Attended by a Skilled Birth Attendant, Percentage, 2012

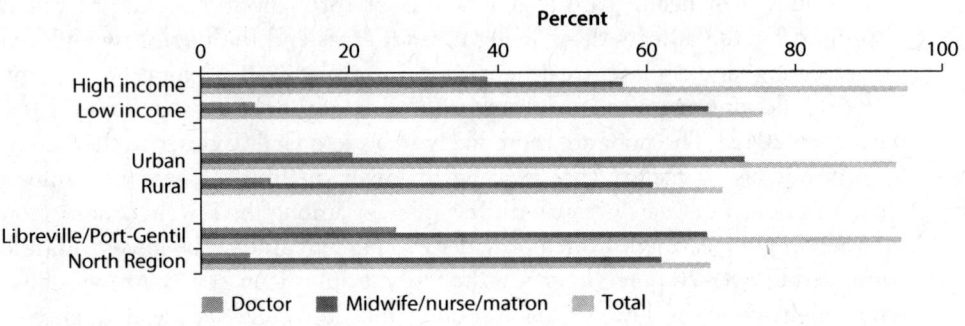

Source: GDHS 2013.

Figure 2.9 Barriers to Accessing Health Care Reported by Women (15–49 years), 2012

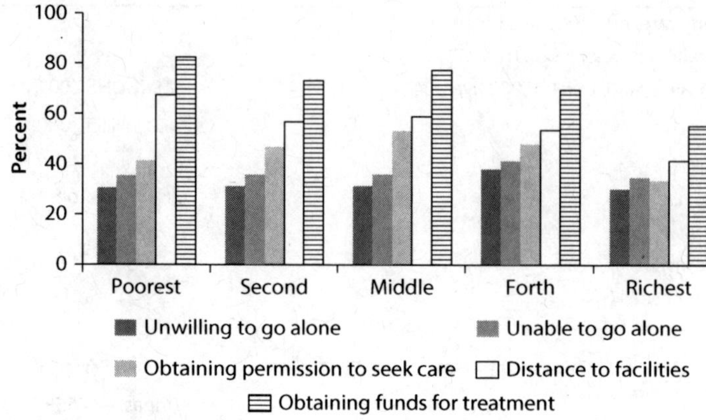

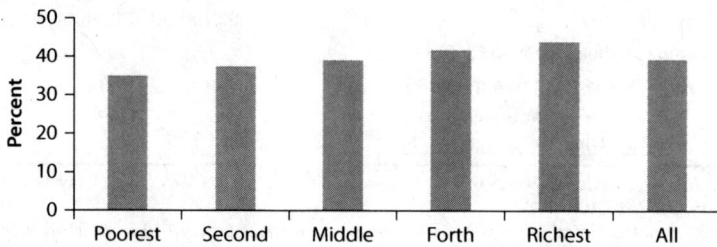

Source: GDHS 2013.

Figure 2.10 Women Receiving All Necessary Exams during Prenatal Visits, Percentage, 2012

Source: GDHS 2013.

in point that cries out for attention (only 37 percent children with diarrhea received oral rehydration therapy, GDHS 2013).

The quality of health care is generally poor throughout the country, but it disproportionately affects those living in rural areas and the poor. Few children are receiving appropriate treatment (for example oral rehydration therapy [ORT]) following an episode of diarrhea (37 percent) or an episode of fever (67 percent in 2012). The poor are more likely to go to a facility closer to their community but also a facility that may be of lower quality. For example, among children under five years of age with fever, fewer among the lower consumption quintile sought treatment from a provider (50 percent among the lowest quintile compared to over 70 percent among the highest quintile in 2011). Among those who sought care, the lowest consumption quintile received a lower quality of care (30 percent among the lowest quintile received antibiotics compared to about 60 percent among the highest quintile in 2011) (figure 2.11).

Where Do the Ill Go for Health Care?

Most of the population relies on public facilities for health care, regardless of their economic status. Most Gabonese women from all economic backgrounds go to the

Figure 2.11 Health Service Use and Quality of Care among Children Under 5 Years of Age with Fever, 2012

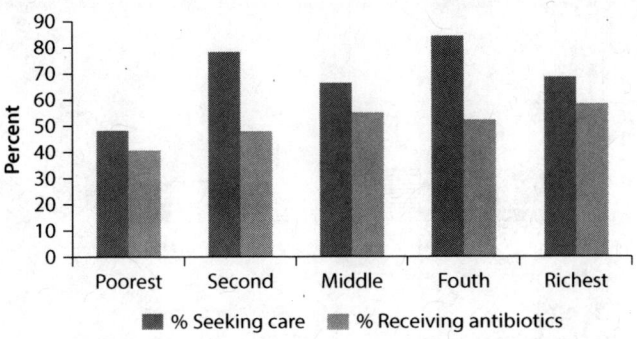

Source: GDHS 2013.

Figure 2.12 Health Facility Attendance by Consumption Quintile

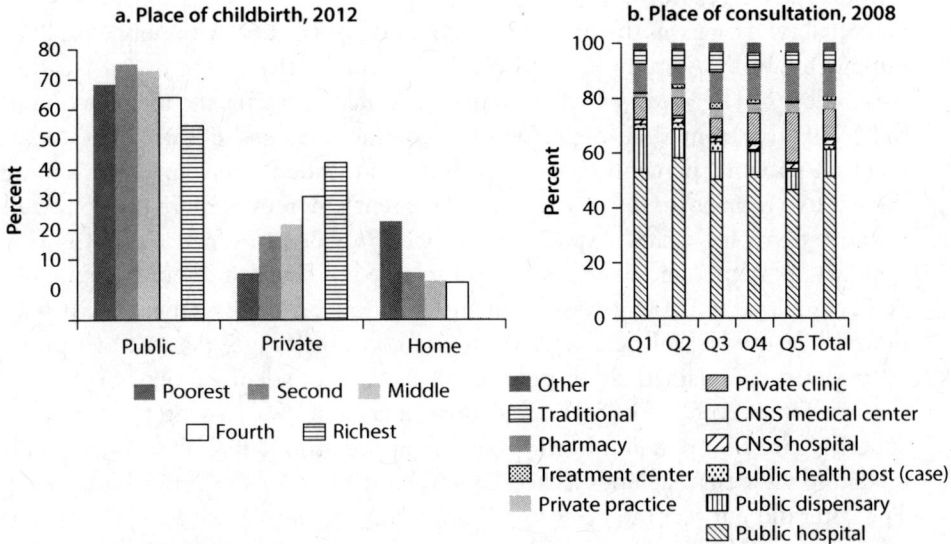

Source: Panel a: GDHS, 2013; Panel b: Direction Générale de la Statistique et des Études Economiques (DGS), *Annuaire Statistique* 2009 (from EGEP).

public sector for childbirth (GDHS 2013). At least one-third of women in the higher consumption quintile use private facilities and at least one-fifth of women in the lowest consumption quintile deliver at home. Among patients using health facilities for consultations, many bypassed lower level facilities; instead they went to public hospitals. That was the case for all consumption quintiles. A public dispensary was more popular among lower consumption quintiles whereas higher consumption quintiles tended to prefer private clinics (EGEP 2009)[8] (figure 2.12).

Figure 2.13 Patient Perceptions and Reasons for Dissatisfaction with Public Facilities during Childbirth, 2000 and 2012

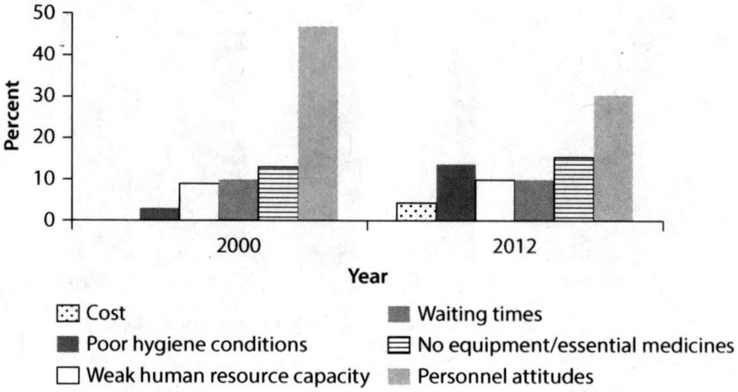

Source: GDHS 2001, 2013.

What Is the Perception on Quality of Care?

Poor quality of care was the primary reason for dissatisfaction with public facilities during childbirth. A study (GDHS 2013) was conducted on the use of facilities for childbirth. The study, which took place several years after the introduction of the NHIP, represented an opportunity to conduct pre- and postprogram assessment on patients' perceptions of services. The attitude of personnel was among the top two reasons for dissatisfaction (30 percent); moreover, more than one-half of the patients felt that the quality of services provided was inadequate (54 percent, 2012). Although fewer persons complained of the attitude of personnel in 2012 compared to 2000, it was still the number one reason for patient dissatisfaction. While the lack of personnel was not a concern (only 2 percent of women interviewed complained about personnel), the lack of adequate personnel was a concern (18 percent). The lack of adequate personnel was among the top three concerns cited by patients from urban areas and from Libreville. Patients also tended to view that facilities lacked equipment (9 percent) or drugs (6 percent). The latter did not seem to be as significant a concern among patients. The lack of equipment and/or drugs was among the top three concerns among patients from rural areas and other cities. Patients did not find waiting time to be much of an issue (10 percent) nor did they find the cost of care to be a concern (4 percent); nevertheless, the cost of care was more of a concern among patients in 2012 than in 2000. However, the cost of care was more of a concern in cities other than Libreville. It was not possible to gather information on quality of care at private facilities. In the future, a facility-based survey could help gather more appropriate information on the quality of care (figure 2.13).

Summary

Life expectancy at birth remains below average compared to countries with similar incomes. Gabon has a higher burden of communicable diseases and disease patterns that is more common in low income countries. In most cases, Gabon remains unable to meet MDG targets for health; their targets for child nutrition are an exception. Inequity in the use of services is rampant; urban residents and the higher consumption quintiles benefit the most.

The country has a hospital-centric health delivery system. Its hospital bed ratio compares to figures seen in Organization for Economic Cooperation and Development (OECD) countries. These countries have a higher disease burden from noncommunicable diseases and an older population. Furthermore, Gabon has inefficiencies; occupancy rates among regional hospitals have been as low as 40 percent. Hospitals are used for primary, secondary, and tertiary care. Using hospitals for primary health care can be expensive for providers and patients. Many resources are inefficiently allocated to hospitals.

Primary health care services are not as widely accessible; they are also under-resourced and lacking in funds for personnel and drugs. Health posts and outreach services that address communicable diseases are not widespread. This state of affairs has resulted in poor use of services for basic health care and in relatively higher and stagnating health outcomes. Under-5 child mortality and maternal mortality are examples.

Gabon has health personnel that meet WHO benchmarks; however, these personnel are not well distributed throughout the country. In addition, accountability systems are weak and staff absenteeism is a problem. Overall, the quality of care is much affected by the lack of qualified staff, especially in lower level facilities and by region. A lack of drugs and medical equipment and the poor attitude and quality of services provided at these facilities also warrants attention and remedy. Among rural patients the cost of care has become more of a concern than it was in the past when public facilities offered free health care to all.

Notes

1. The National Health Development Plan (PNDS 2011–15), stated MMR was 520 per 100,000 childbirths in 2010. WHO (Gabon Health Statistics Profile 2010) states MMR to be 260 in 2008.

2. WHO, United Nations Children's Fund (UNICEF), United Nations Population Fund (UNFPA), World Bank estimates. 2011. Trends in maternal mortality 1990–2010.

3. Data are from GDHS, 2013. Definition of wasting: Moderate and severe—below minus two standard deviations from median weight for height of reference population. UNICEF. http://www.unicef.org/infobycountry/stats_popup2.html

4. WHO. http://www.who.int/healthinfo/global_burden_disease/estimates_regional/en/

5. United Nations Program on HIV/AIDS (UNAIDS) Global Report 2013 http://www.unaids.org/en/media/unaids/contentassets/documents/epidemiology/2013/gr2013/UNAIDS_Global_Report_2013_en.pdf

6. UNAIDS.

7. DOTS is directly observed treatment, short-course (for tuberculosis).

8. Enquête Gabonaise sur l'Evaluation et le suivi de la Pauvreté.

CHAPTER 3

Health Financing

Introduction

This chapter offers a perspective on health financing in Gabon as compared to other countries with similar incomes. It also provides insight on how health spending has changed over time, including financing from the public and the private (out-of-pocket) spending, as well as a perspective on allocative efficiency on public spending for health.

Key Findings

- Gabon's health spending as a share of gross domestic product (GDP) (3.5 percent in 2012) is lower than average when compared to countries within the region and countries of similar income.
- Health spending in the public sector as a share of GDP (1.7 percent in 2012) and as a share of total health spending (51 percent in 2012) is also lower, than averages seen in countries of similar income and in countries within the region.
- Gabon's per capita total health spending (PPP$ 558 or $397 in 2012) is significantly higher than neighboring countries. However, it is slightly below average when compared to other countries of similar income.
- Household out-of-pocket as share of total health spending is relatively high (41 percent in 2012) and it shows little evidence of offering financial protection against the costs associated with illness.
- Overall, health spending has grown. The public sector contributes at least one-half of total health spending, due in part to the introduction of Caisse Nationale d'Assurance Maladie et de Garantie Sociale (National Health Insurance and Social Security; CNAMGS).
- Budget execution rates in the public sector for health have been at unacceptable levels.
- There are concerns about allocative inefficiency in the public sector for health. Much of public health resources in Gabon go for curative care and to hospitals.

- Over time, capital investment as a share of the budget has crept upward. In recent years it has represented about 40 percent of total public sector health spending.
- At least one-half of recurrent health spending goes for personnel. Additionally, some off-budget also gets allocated to personnel.
- Over time, on-budget resources for "operations" appear to have declined; meanwhile, off-budget resources for "operations" have grown.
- The geographic distribution of health resources is inequitable and does not reflect the real needs of the people.

Global Comparisons

Gabon does not fare well when its health spending patterns are compared to other countries of similar income. As a share of GDP, Gabon spent about 3.5 percent in 2012. That was well below the Sub-Saharan Africa regional average (6.2 percent) and below the average of countries with similar income (6.1 percent). On the other hand, in 2012 Gabon's health spending per capita was about $397 (or PPP[1] $558), which was significantly higher than neighboring countries (PPP$153). However, Gabon spends slightly below average when compared to other countries of similar income (PPP$602) (figure 3.1).

The public sector's health spending patterns do not fare well either. As a share of GDP, Gabon's public sector's spending for health (1.7 percent in 2012) is lower than countries of similar income. Based on its per capita spending for health in the public sector, the country also does not fare well when compared to countries of similar income (figure 3.2).

As a share of total government spending (7.2 percent, 2012), Gabon spends below the regional average (9 percent) and below average when compared to countries of similar income (11 percent). As a share of total health expenditure (THE, 51 percent, 2012), the public share is also below average when compared to countries of similar income (Figure 3.3 and appendix A).

Gabon's investment in health lags behind most countries in upper-middle-income country (UMIC) and it trails many African Countries. As a matter of policy, the country has placed a higher priority on economic "production" sectors over social sectors. Despite a significant budget surplus from 2005–09, most of that surplus went to the reduction of foreign debt.

Households bear much of the burden for health care costs. The percentage of total health spending spent by household out-of-pocket (OOP) is relatively high (41 percent, 2012). There is scant evidence that households have financial protection against illness costs.[2] According to a benchmark by the World Health Organization (WHO), out-of-pocket (OOP) spending for health should not exceed 15–20 percent of a country's total health

Figure 3.1 Total Health Spending as Compared to Other Countries with Similar Income

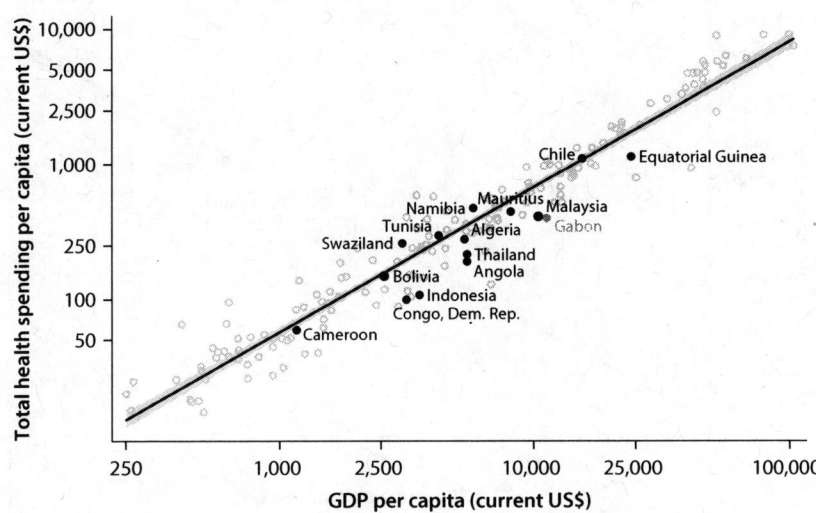

a. Per capita health spending, US$

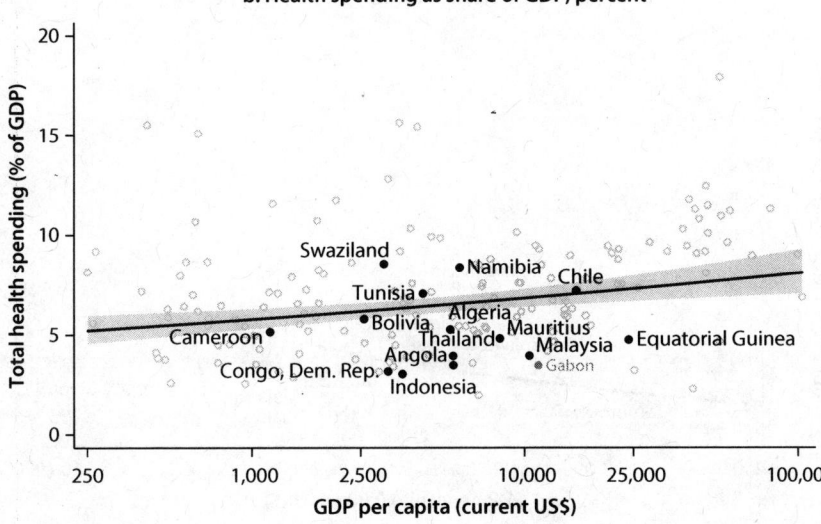

b. Health spending as share of GDP, percent

Source: World Bank.
Note: GDP = gross domestic product.

expenditures. Gabon falls short of this benchmark. Its data show that its share of OOP health spending remains above 40 percent of total health expenditures (figure 3.4).

A global benchmarking exercise was conducted using information from national health accounts (WHO). The findings demonstrate that Gabon's OOP health spending (per capita and as a share of GDP) is average when compared

Figure 3.2 Public Health Spending Compared to Countries with Similar Income

a. Per capita health spending, US$

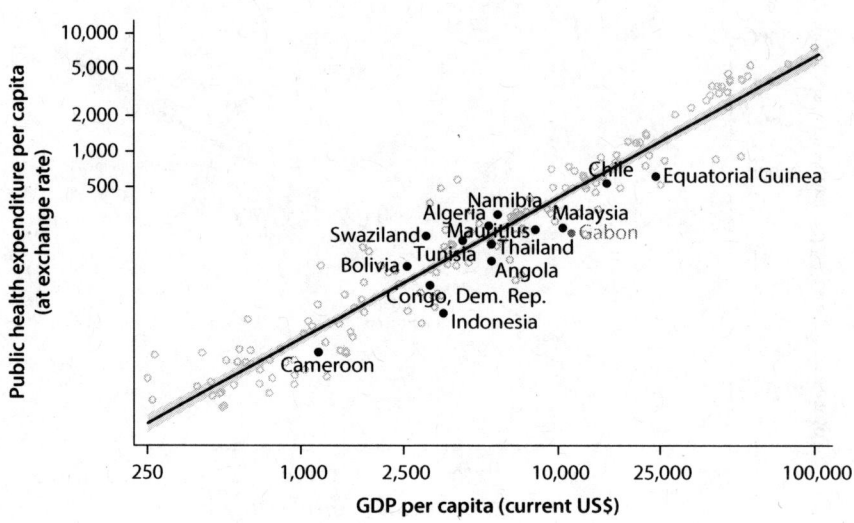

b. Public health spending as share of GDP, percent

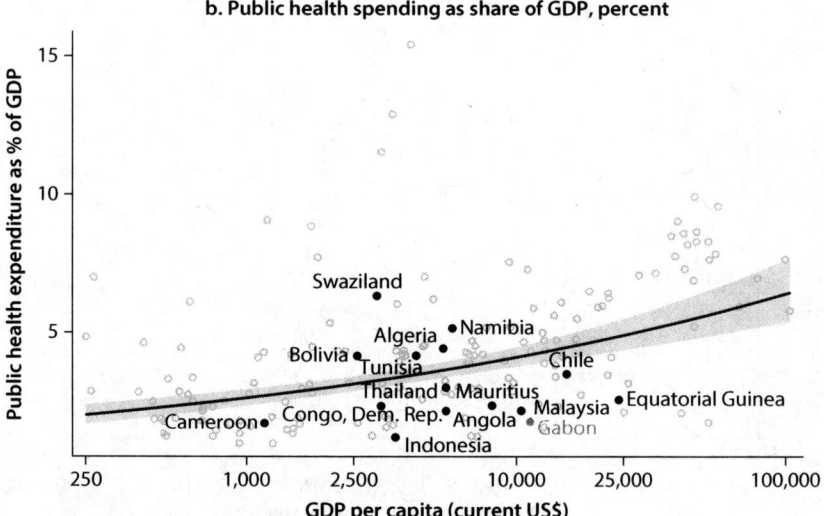

Source: World Development Indicators, WHO, updated in Apr 2014.
Note: x–axis log scale. Gray area indicates 95% confidence interval for the fitted line.

to the other countries of similar income. This shows that many countries of similar income also have a challenge in providing financial protection to its population (figure 3.5).

Figure 3.3 Public Health Spending Shares Compared to Other Countries of Similar Income

a. As a share of total health spending

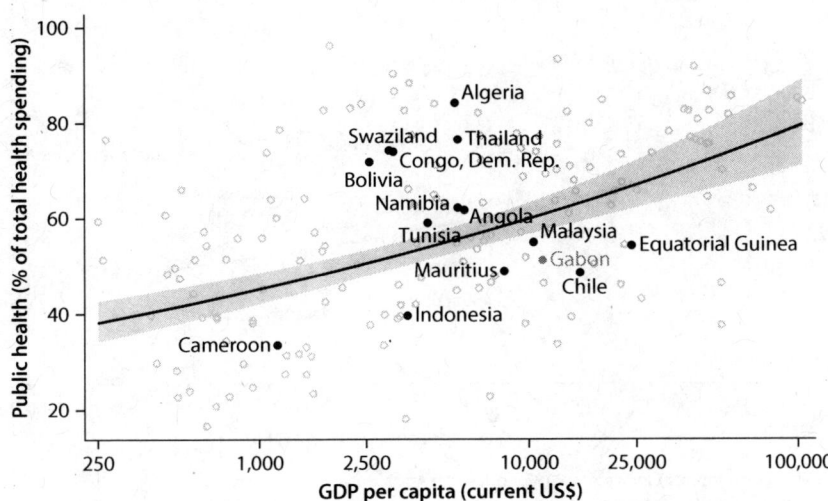

b. As a share of total government spending

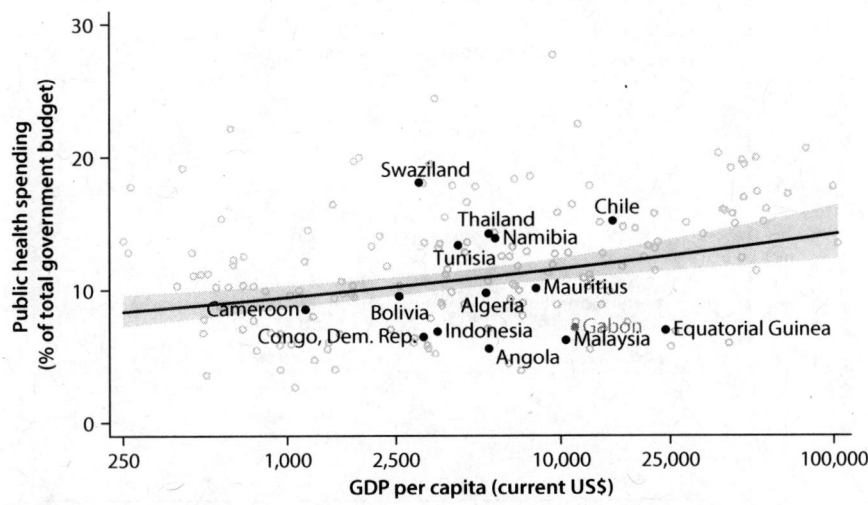

Source: World Development Indicators, WHO, updated in Apr 2014.
Note: x–axis log scale. Gray area indicates 95% confidence interval for the fitted line.

Figure 3.4 Out-of-Pocket Health Spending as a Share of Total Health Spending Compared to Countries with Similar Income

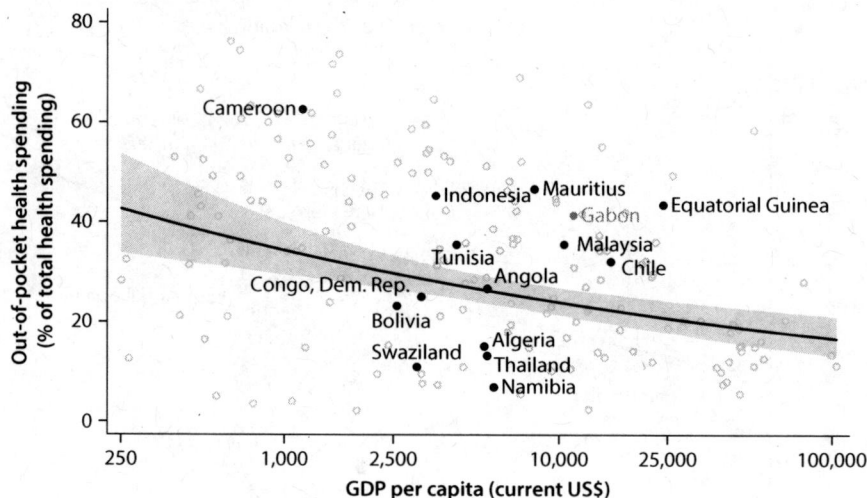

Source: World Development Indicators, WHO, updated in Apr 2014.
Note: x–axis log scale. Gray area indicates 95% confidence interval for the fitted line.

Figure 3.5 Out-of-Pocket Health Spending Compared to Countries with Similar Income

a. Per capita health spending, US$

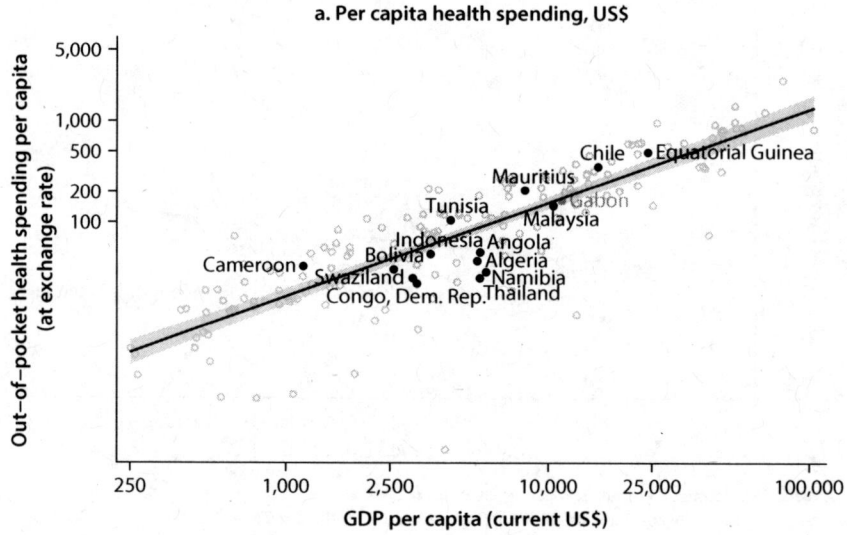

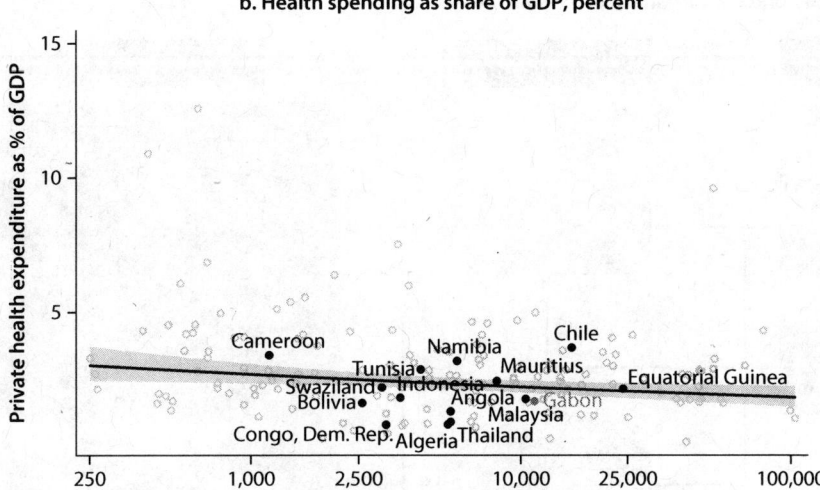

b. Health spending as share of GDP, percent

Source: World Development Indicators, WHO, updated in Apr 2014.
Note: x–axis log scale. Gray area indicates 95% confidence interval for the fitted line.

Health Financing Functions

In the absence of a comprehensive National Health Accounts study for Gabon, mapping the flow of resources can only be approximate. The chief conclusion is that health facilities receive flows from almost every major source—without any pooling of funds (CNAMGS is supposed to gradually fill this role). Ministry of Health and Public Hygiene (MOHPH) does not manage all public facilities and funds: other ministries (especially Defense) have parallel and independent structures (figure 3.6).

Sources of Health Financing

Funding of the Gabonese health system comes from three main sources: (i) the government budget; (ii) health insurance contributions by employers and employees (including the National Health Insurance Program [NHIP]—CNAMGS, and some private insurers); and (iii) out-of-pocket expenditures by households.

A positive trend in total health spending has occurred over the past decade. In the past decade, THE increased from 2.5 percent of GDP in 2000 to 3.5 percent of GDP in 2012; it increased 250 percent to reach $451 Million in 2010.[3] After 2008 the growth in spending was due to an increase in government spending but mainly to the expansion of the NHIP. Most likely, that growth would have continued after 2010 to reach a projected $500 Million in 2013. Over the past decade, the composition of THE has gradually changed, particularly during

Figure 3.6 Flow of Funds in the Gabonese Health Sector

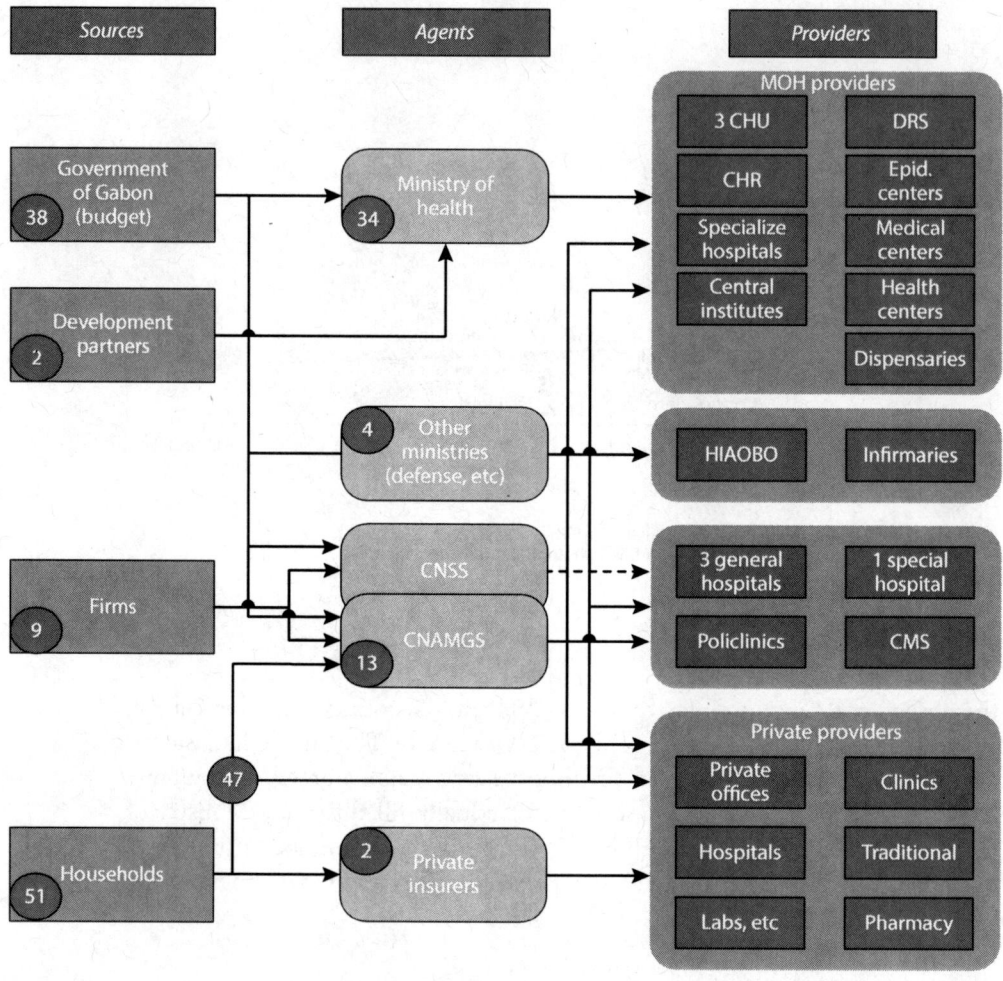

Source: World Bank. Numbers in circles represent the approximate proportion of total funding accounted for by each source, agency or flow.
Note: CHU is Centre Hospitalier Universitaire, DRS is Direction Generale de Santé, CHR is Centre Hospitalier Regional, HIABOB is Hopital d'Instruction des Armées Omar Bongo Ondimba, CMS is Centre Médicaux-Sociaux, CNAMGS is Caisse Nationale d'Assurance Maladie et Solidarité, CNSS is Caisse Nationale de Sécurité Sociale.

2006/07 and in the last two years (2011/12). Growth accelerated because of government spending for NHIP (figure 3.7 and 3.8).

Since 2008, overall health spending has grown even though total health spending plummeted to 2.7 percent of GDP as a result of the global economic and financial crisis. However, when compared to a longer period (since 1995), health's share of GDP has more or less remained stable at around 3.4–3.5 percent. Because of the public sector's commitment to health during this time, their share grew from 36 percent of total health spending in 1995 to 51 percent of total health spending in 2012. Government health spending, became the largest contributor to Gabon's THE in 2012. With the establishment of CNAMGS,

Figure 3.7 Trends in Total and Public Per Capita Health Spending over Time

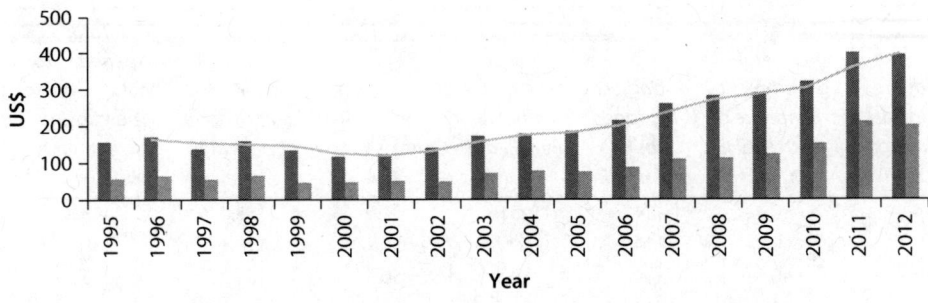

Source: WHO, National Health Accounts, 2013.

Figure 3.8 Trends in the Level and Composition of Total Health Expenditure

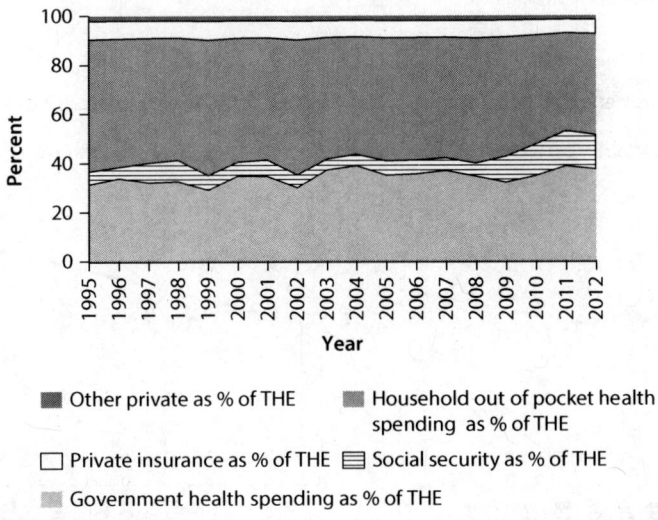

Source: WHO, National Health Accounts, 2013.
Note: THE = total health expenditure.

overall resources for health have increased from $283 per capita in 2008 to $397 in 2012 in nominal terms (National Health Accounts [NHA], WHO). In 2012, CNAMGS received 14 percent of total health spending or 27 percent of public health spending (table 3.1).

Gabon does not meet the Abuja target. As a proportion of general government expenditures for health, Gabon allocates about 7.2 percent: social security contributions represent about 27 percent of this amount (data is for 2012, NHA, WHO 2013). Although the country has shown a greater commitment to health (the government budget increased from about 5.5 percent in 2008 to 7.2 percent in 2012), that percentage experienced considerable volatility over the years; it still remains below the Abuja commitment[4] (figure 3.9).

Table 3.1 Health Spending, 1995–2012

Year	Total health expenditure (THE) % gross domestic product (GDP)	General government expenditure on health (GGHE) as % of THE	Social security funds as % of GGHE	Private expenditure on health (PvtHE) as % of THE	Out-o- pocket expenditure as % of THE	Total expenditure on health/capita at exchange rate	Total expenditure on health/capita at purchasing power parity (NCU per US$)
1995	3.4	36.4	14.5	63.6	54.0	158.0	418.8
2000	2.9	40.3	14.2	59.7	50.7	118.1	338.5
2005	3.0	40.7	14.4	59.3	50.3	187.2	385.3
2006	3.2	41.0	13.5	59.0	50.1	216.0	421.6
2007	3.3	41.9	12.3	58.1	49.3	261.6	457.5
2008	2.7	39.7	13.5	60.3	51.2	283.4	376.3
2009	3.7	42.5	24.9	57.5	48.8	291.3	493.6
2010	3.5	47.4	27.1	52.6	44.6	322.4	490.7
2011	3.4	52.9	27.1	47.1	40.0	401.4	516.4
2012	3.5	51.2	27.1	48.8	41.4	396.7	558.2

Source: National Health Accounts, World Health Organization.
Note: NCU = national currency unit.

Figure 3.9 Government Health Budget as a Share of the Total Government Budget

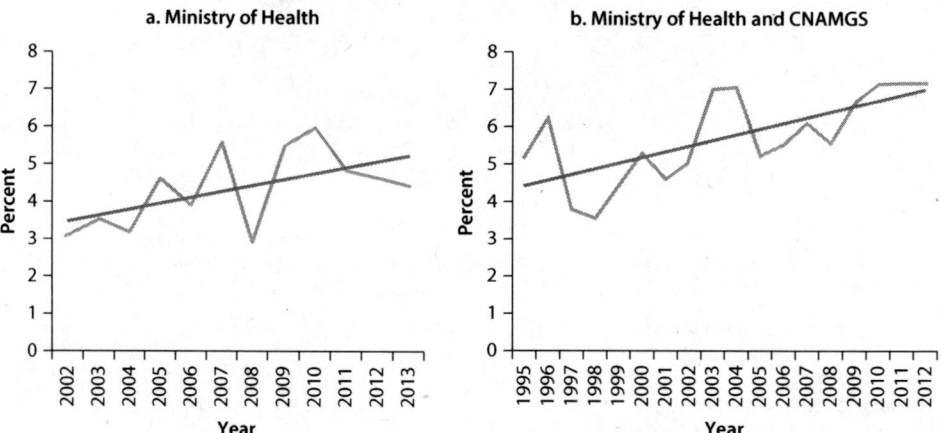

Source: Panel a: Gabon, Ministry of Budget, 2013; Panel b: National Health Accounts, WHO, 2014.
Note: Various sources of data provided different information. NHA provides a more comprehensive picture of public spending for health; NHA's goes beyond that of MOHPH.

Budget execution rates have been low. In 2010, budget execution was just above 70 percent, but it was reported to be much lower in preceding years. However, in recent years, the government has made an attempt to improve its budget execution for health. Despite these efforts, poor budget planning has impeded an improvement in its performance (figure 3.10).

Figure 3.10 Budget Execution in the Health Sector, Percent, 2002–11

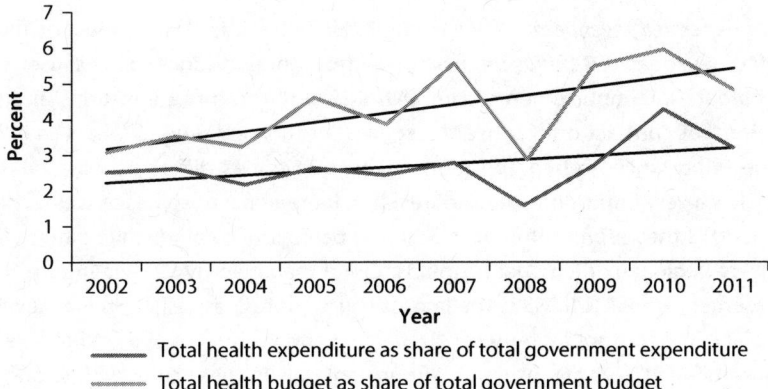

a. Health budget/expenditure as share of total
government budget/expenditure, percent

Total health expenditure as share of total government expenditure

Total health budget as share of total government budget

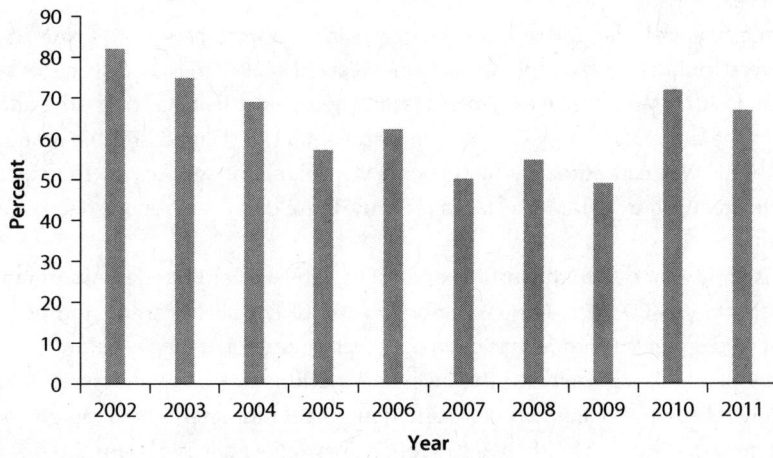

b. Share of health budget spent, percent

Source: Ministry of Budget. World Bank based on the audit report on social
spending on hospitals in Gabon.

Internally Generated Revenue (IGR)

Off-budget revenue (reimbursement from CNAMGS and others[5]) has become
critical in the financing of operations at health facilities. These resources help with
the purchase of drugs (those not financed under the budget), and with staff incentives. Regulations indicate how much of these earnings the facility may retain and
how much are to be pooled under the treasury. Regulations also exist on what
portion of retained earnings may be used for staff incentives and what portion
may be used for facility operations. However, these regulations are not enforced;
furthermore, not all facilities comply with them in a consistent manner (box 3.1).

Box 3.1 The Case of Lambarene Regional Hospital (CHR Georges Rawiri)—Regional Hospital for the Center Health Region (Moyen-Ogooue Province)—Evidence from Comanaged CHR

Internally generated revenue at the Regional Hospital: Facilities "own funds" or Internally Generated Revenues/IGR (*fonds propres*) come from three distinct sources: user charges (*recettes propres*), reimbursements from CNAMGS and from private insurers and private companies that contract out for health services for their employees (*prises en charge* or PEC). The importance and composition of these revenues differs by hospital. On the whole, IGR is a very important source of revenue for regional hospitals as well as other facilities; in 2012 they represented from 32 to 50 percent of total revenue among Centres Hospitaliers Régionaux (Regional hospitals; CHRs) managed by VAMED (figure B3.1.1b). Reimbursement from CNAMGS is the largest source of IGR, especially in Franceville. This form of IGR could account for between 16 percent and 32 percent of the total revenue for these hospitals. PEC (private insurers) is important only in those cities with strong formal economic activity (Franceville, Port Gentil in addition to the capital). User charges, although still important (between 9 percent and 23 percent of the total), is declining as CNAMGS expands.

On the financial side, the report cites delays in reimbursement from CNAMGS. It can take several months. For example, an amount received in 2012 may actually be for services rendered in 2011. Moreover, even when a facility gets paid, there may be a large difference between the amount paid by CNAMGS and the amounts claimed and the amounts expected. (This was computed by multiplying the volume of services by the current fee schedule practiced by CNAMGS).[6] More recently, these delays are reported to be less of a problem.

IGR is important due to the insufficiency of the government budget. According to the same report (VAMED 2012 Annual Report on the CHRs), since contracting began, the amount paid under the budget has been consistently and substantially below the amount originally planned, especially for the investment budget. As a result, hospitals have increasingly relied on IGR; infrastructure and equipment has deteriorated rapidly. And yet, the differences identified by the VAMED report may reflect a lack of transparency in payment methods.

The report also documents the existence of wide differences between the amounts claimed and those received from CNAMGS; to a lesser extent, other insurers have had a similar experience (figure B3.1.1a). In addition, amounts received do not necessarily reflect amounts accounted for or recorded by the Central Treasury. The large, unexplained differences in these funds and the delays in receiving them, which vary greatly from one facility to another, are evidence of serious issues of control and transparency at the various system levels for managing IGRs. In general, they contribute to a lack of predictability of facility funding. The cause of these problems may stem from a weak claims filing process on the facility side unclear or poor practices for analyzing and auditing claims on the side of insurers, or both. Although, CNAMGS is said to have improved this situation; nevertheless, it is important enough to deserve further scrutiny.

box continues next page

Box 3.1 The Case of Lambarene Regional Hospital (CHR Georges Rawiri)—Regional Hospital for the Center Health Region (Moyen-Ogooue Province)—Evidence from Comanaged CHR *(continued)*

Figure B3.1.1 Composition of Total Revenue by Source in Comanaged CHRs, 2012

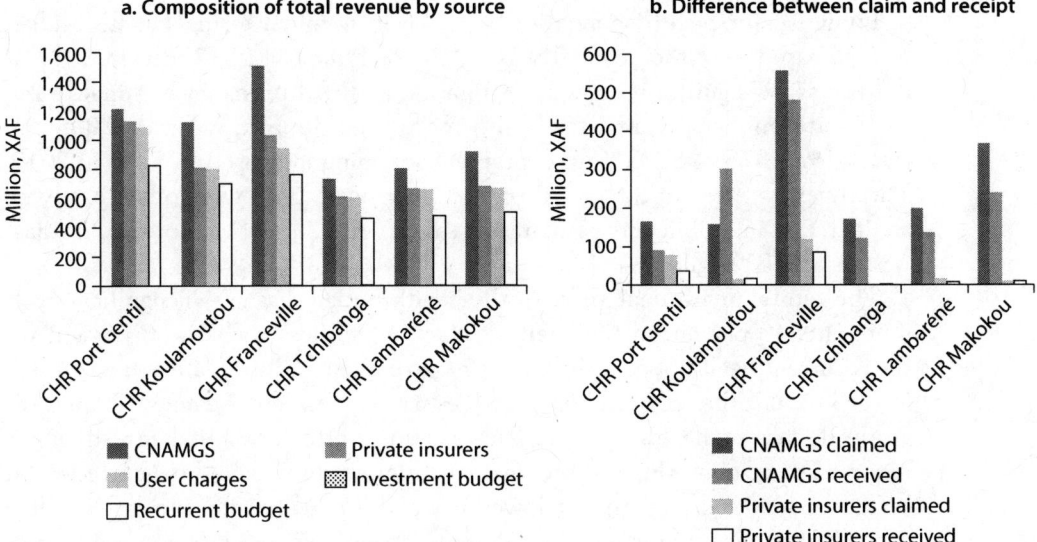

a. Composition of total revenue by source

b. Difference between claim and receipt

Legend (left):
- CNAMGS
- User charges
- Recurrent budget
- Private insurers
- Investment budget

Legend (right):
- CNAMGS claimed
- CNAMGS received
- Private insurers claimed
- Private insurers received

Source: VAMED Annual Financial Report 2012.
Note: CHR = Centres Hospitaliers Régionaux; CNAMGS = Caisse Nationale d´Assurance Maladie et de Garantie Sociale; XAF = Central Africa CFA Francs.

Spending Patterns for Public Financing for Health

Budgeting processes in Gabon are historical and incremental, rather than based on outputs. The country has a central budget, with limited control given to sectors over wage bills and government employment. Because of the lack of a sound upstream budget regulatory system, arrears tend to accumulate. Audit services are deficient and there are discrepancies between budget execution and physical execution. Budget implementation suffers from procedures that undermine fiscal discipline. Computerized procedures for executing the budget are lacking, especially controls over decentralized levels (World Bank 2012b). The government plans to move to an output-based budgeting process. Some sectors, including MOHPH, are at the head of the line when the new process goes into effect during the 2015/16 budget cycle. MOHPH completed the development of the National Health Development Plan (PNDS), 2011–15. That has put MOHPH in a favorable position to implement its budget based on a program objective. To do so, MOHPH will need to: (i) establish an annual system for monitoring–evaluating the implementation of PNDS, and (ii) during the transitional period present its budget under both the traditional method and the budget per program objective method (World Bank 2012b). A Bank project is working with several ministries to strengthen their public financial management capacity. That includes preparing procurement plans, information systems and building capacity for budget monitoring-evaluation. However, MOHPH lacks the capacity and systems to move toward a program objective method of budgeting.

Public sector health spending has grown in nominal terms. Health budget has increased over the years; it was XAF 128 billion in 2012. But in 2012, it did not show significant growth in nominal and real terms. In nominal terms, per capita public spending for health more than doubled between 2005 and 2012 (from $76 to $203); per capita real spending increased to $124 in 2012. The adverse effects of the global economic crisis of 2008 were offset partly by an increase in public investment that began in 2009 (Maino and Troujas-Bernate 2013) (figure 3.11).

The capital investment share of the health budget has grown significantly. It represents 40 percent of the health budget, which leaves about 60 percent for the recurrent health budget. However, recurrent expenditures are actually much lower. In 2012, the recurrent expenditures were reported to be below 70 percent of the recurrent health budget. The execution rate for capital investment is reported to be above 80 percent; the execution rate for the nonsalary recurrent budget is reported to be much lower. About 20 percent of recurrent spending goes for medicine and medical supplies: two-thirds of that amount is for drugs and one-third is for medical supplies (Ministry of Budget 2013). Other recurrent budget items (*solde permanente*, *agents de la main d'oeuvre non* [MONP] and others) are reportedly not being disbursed. There is no explanation for this—except that it could be due to an insufficient budget formulation and preparation process and a lack of budget execution tools such as for procurement (World Bank). Therefore, health facilities are likely to rely on off-budget earnings, such as IGR, for their operations.

Figure 3.11 Per Capita Public Sector Health Spending in Nominal and Real Terms, 2005–12

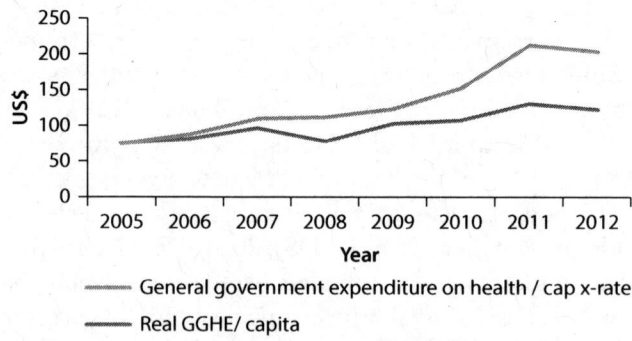

Source: WHO, NHA, 2013.
Note: Base year is 2005. http://apps.who.int/nha/database/DataExplorer.
aspx?ws=2&d=1. GGHE = general government health expenditure.

Capital Investment

Over time, capital investment as a share of the budget has crept upward. In 2012, 40 percent of budget went to capital health spending. The rationale: to support the objectives under the Growth Poverty Reduction Strategy (GPRS) (2006) that included improving the population's access to basic social services.[7] Based on the experience of other countries, in general, capital investments take up a smaller portion of the budget, usually in the range of 10–20 percent (figure 3.12).

Personnel Spending

At least half of recurrent health spending goes for personnel.[8] On-budget recurrent spending pays for personnel remuneration and operations. However, there appears to be a demand to recruit additional (temporary) contractual staff outside the budget. The Ministry of Budget has added a line item under the nonsalary recurrent budgets as *agents de la main d'oeuvre non permanente* (MONP). This line item refers to nonpermanent workers or daily workers paid directly by MOHPH. For 2012, the amount budgeted was XAF 5 billion or about 7 percent of the nonsalary recurrent budget.

Basic staff remuneration in the public sector is low relative to parapublic and private staff remuneration.[9] Salary levels also favor urban over rural centers.[10] However, personnel working in public health facilities receive several additional amounts based on their location, working hours, function or responsibility. In addition, an incentive bonus is paid monthly; the amount is substantial in comparison to the base wage. Facilities pay these bonuses out of the IGR collected. In the absence of regulations from MOHPH, facilities have applied their own interpretations of the law on the use of IGR and on bonuses.

Figure 3.12 Public Budget for Health, 2002–13

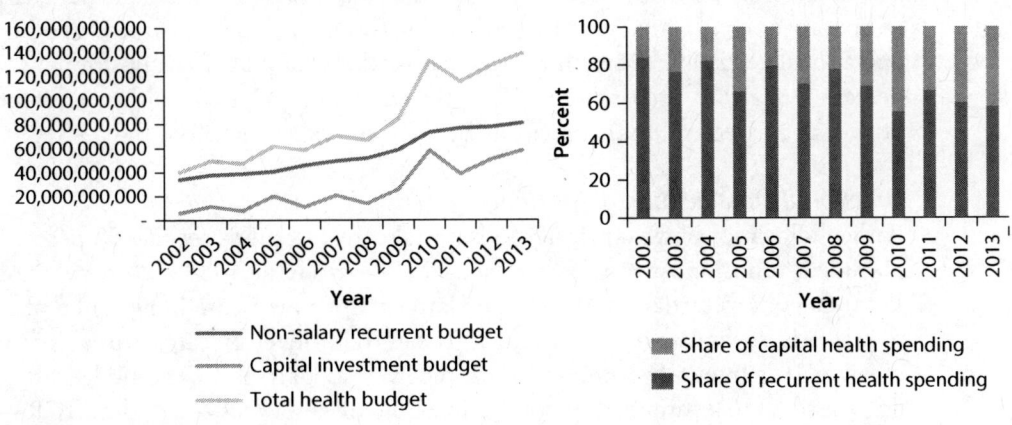

Source: Ministry of Budget.
Note: All data are budgets and not actual expenditures.

Box 3.2 The Case of Kango Medical Center in the West Health Region (Estuaire Province)

Staffing: Both the level and allocation of financial resources are inadequate. Resources available for 2012 amounted to XAF 62 million or $ 6.08 per capita. Budget allocations accounted for 77 percent of the total. Transfers from the Central Drugs Office (*Office Pharmaceutique National*) amounted to 16 percent; the total of government resources was 93 percent. Internally generated revenue/IGR (*fonds propres*) accounted for 7 percent. Seventy-six percent of total funding (but 91 percent of the budget) went to personnel (permanent and temporary). That included 3 percent for staff incentives which were funded by IGR. Temporary staff spending consumed 35 percent of the total allocation, nearly one-half of total expenditures for staff.

Source: World Bank's personal visit, interviews with staff and review of records.

Off-budget pays for the salaries of temporary staff and for staff bonuses/ incentives. Staff are likely to benefit from incentives because of off-budget earnings. However, the current staff incentives (bonuses) are (i) not performance based, and (ii) not aligned with performance. Therefore, there is little incentive for staff to change their behavior and strengthen the delivery of service for these programs. Performance-based payment interventions have led to better and more targeted results, by triggering: (i) staff motivation, (ii) accountability, (iii) monitoring, (iv) goal orientation, and (v) performance based rewards/recognition. There is an opportunity to realign incentives with performance and improve the quality of care for maternal and child health as well as preventive care (box 3.2).

Operations Spending

Over time, on-budget resources for "operations" appear to be on the decline. Meanwhile, there is a growing reliance on off-budget resources for "operations." The recurrent budget is allocated for (i) *solde permanente* or permanent staff, (ii) temporary or contractual staff, (iii) medicines, (iv) medical supplies, and (v) other operational costs. The shares for drugs and medical supplies went up from 12.5 percent in 2010 to 19 percent in 2012; the share for operations in the recurrent budget decreased from 29 percent in 2010 to 26 percent in 2012 (box 3.3).

Functional Classification of the Budget

Budget allocations give a priority to hospital care. Hospitals receive 58 percent of budget funds; most of it goes to secondary regional hospitals, 20 percent of the total goes to tertiary hospitals. The latter is apt to increase in light of a plan to upgrade several regional hospitals to a tertiary-level of care. Primary care receives 16 percent and public health receives 13 percent of the budget. It is not possible to estimate the total allocation of resources—including IGR— because no consolidated IGR data are available. But it is probably safe to assume that hospitals are the greatest recipients of IGR. For example, at a

Box 3.3 The Case of Kango Medical Center in the West Health Region (Estuaire Province)

Operations: Apart from drugs, the allocation for nonstaff operational expenses are minimal (8 percent). Most of the funding comes from IGR. There is no budget allocation for maintenance, staff clothing or lab consumables; the allocation for drugs is insufficient. The release of funds is often delayed, which can lead to critical bottlenecks and service interruptions. IGR is an important source of revenues, but the revenue tends to be much lower than its potential due to unclear exemption policies[11] and the poverty of many residents. Revenue from CNAMGS is limited. Because no tools or guidelines are in place, monitoring IGR is weak.

Source: World Bank's personal visit, interviews with staff and review of records.

Figure 3.13 Budget Allocation by Level and Facility Type, 2011–12

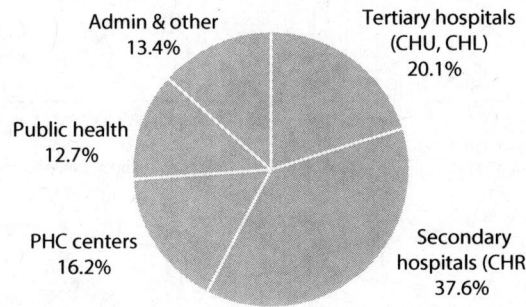

Source: Estimated from budget data.
Note: PHC = primary health care; CHR = Centres Hospitaliers Régionaux; CHU = Centre Hospitalier Universitaire.

regional hospital, IGR may constitute as much as 32–50 percent of its financing. If these funds and flows are inconsistent and/or are delayed, facility operations could be in jeopardy (figure 3.13).

Allocative efficiency is a concern. Eighty percent of the budget goes for curative care and 20 percent for preventive care (PNDS 2011–15 2010). Based on a comparison of the mean number of beds as well as staff and budget allocations across facility types, a substantially higher budget allocation relative to size goes to tertiary level hospitals and a smaller allocation to primary health care (PHC) facilities with beds (Medical Centers) or without beds. The mean budget allocation does not include off-budgetary funds (that is IGR from CNAMGS or user fees) (table 3.2).

If the hospital bed occupancy rate improved and economies of scale went into effect, per capita spending could be reduced. Given the low utilization of hospital beds in several regional hospitals, a significant amount of resources goes to running these facilities. For example, on average, about XAF 22

Table 3.2 Numbers and Features of Different Facility Types

XAF, million

	Number	Mean # beds	Mean staff	Mean annual budget[a]
Tertiary/referral				
CHU (Teaching hospitals[b])	3	246	NA	3,385.72
-CHU Libreville		380	NA	3,744.87
-CHU Angondjé		168	NA	1,690.11
-Army hospital (HIA)		191	NA	4,722.19
Secondary level				
CHR (Regional hospitals)	9	121	208	1,207.19
Specialized hospitals	4	29	64	238.64
Private hospitals	5	83	NA	549.66
-Albert Schweitzer		159	NA	900.00
-Bongolo		142	NA	400.00
Primary level				
Medical centers	40	26	6.5	32.07
Health centers	31	0	29[c]	21.49
SMI (M&CH centers)	12	0	6.3	30.31
Dispensaries	488	0	0.5	0.17

Source: Ministry of Health/Cellule d'Observation de la Santé Publique (Observation Unit of Public Health; COSP).
Note: CHU = Centre Hospitalier Universitaire.
a. Mean recurrent budget allocation for 2011–12, in Million XAF; amount for private hospitals is for the government subsidy alone.
b. Includes the Army Hospital (HIAOBO).
c. Mean staff is 81 in Libreville but 8.5 in the provinces.

million ($40,000)[12] is spent on each bed that is used. This amount could be reduced by about one-half (XAF 10 million) if the hospital had a bed occupancy rate of 100 percent. However, the broader question is: does Gabon need all of its hospital beds? Is there a need to reduce the burden of unused hospital beds? If so, what is the ideal number of hospital beds needed in a country like Gabon with its burden of disease pattern? The country could consider developing a hospital rationalization plan to strengthen its health delivery system (figure 3.14).

Equity in Resource Allocation

The geographic distribution of health resources is inequitable and does not reflect the actual needs of the people, based on population size, poverty or disease burden and assuming the epidemiological profile is similar across the country. Funds, personnel and technical resources are concentrated in urban areas and certain provinces. To some extent, this is inevitable in a country with low population density, a poor road network and a population that is 86 percent urban. But available evidence suggests that these observed inequalities go beyond the constraints of geography and demographics. On a per capita basis, availability of funding and technical staff varies greatly across provinces and departments—for no apparent reason.[13]

Figure 3.14 Per Capita Spending Per Hospital Bed and Per Utilized Bed, 2012

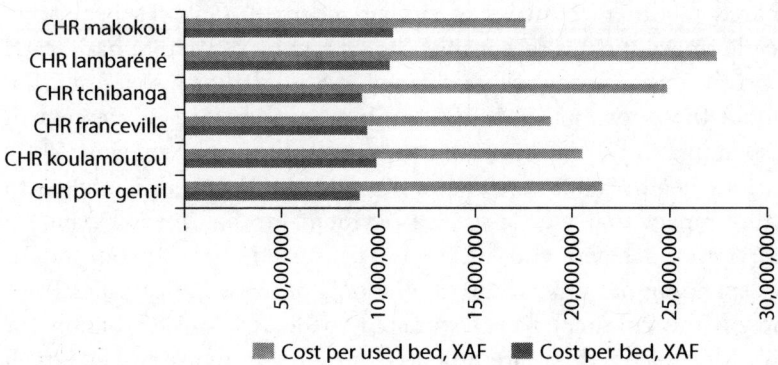

Source: Computed from Ministry of Health/COSP data.
Note: CHR = Centres Hospitaliers Régionaux; XAF = Central Africa CFA Francs.

Figure 3.15 Decentralized Public Expenditure by Region, Hospital Care and PHC, 2012

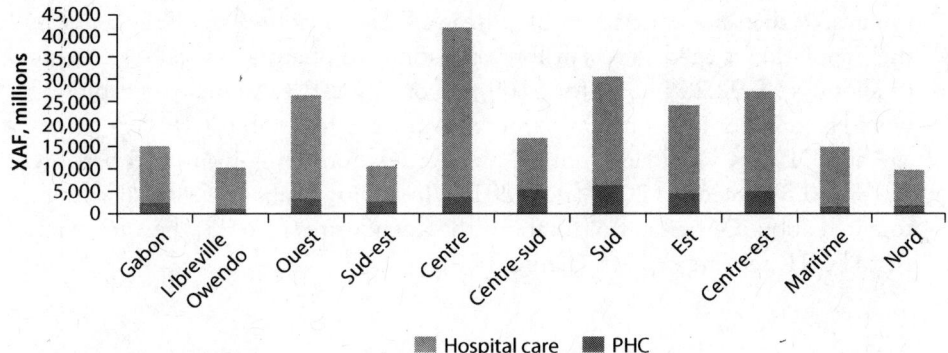

Source: Computed from Budget data (Average Budget for 2010–11, Loi de Finances) and 2008
population data (MOH/COSP).
Note: PHC = primary health care.

Geographic inequalities in funding allocations are large. Although Libreville-
Owendo accounts for 39 percent of the population, it receives only 26.5 percent
of facility-level expenditure for hospitals, Regional health directorates (DRS) and
PHC facilities.[14] On a per capita basis, the recurrent budget allocation for both
primary health care and hospitals varies substantially by region; the ratio is 1:5.
For hospital care, spending is highest in the Centre, South (Sud) and West
(Ouest) Region. Primary health care spending is highest in South (Sud), South
Central (Centre-Sud) and East Central (Centre-Est). Funding allocation appears
to be based on the capacity that is in place rather than need (as proxied by population size). Per capita spending in the capital is significantly lower than the
national average (figure 3.15).

Health Financing in the Republic of Gabon • http://dx.doi.org/10.1596/978-1-4648-0289-8

Pharmaceutical Spending

When compared to other countries of similar income,[15] Gabon's per capita spending for pharmaceutical is reasonable. On an annual per capita basis, total (public and private) pharmaceutical sales were $88 in 2013; s a share of GDP they were about 0.55 percent (BMI 2014). Drugs represented 24 percent of total health spending in 2013. This figure appears to have gone up since 2009 when the various health schemes came under CNAMGS. There is a need to understand the impact that fee-for-service payment mechanism is having on provider prescription behavior and if there is a cause and effect relationship to drug use and spending patterns. In 2013, Gabon's pharmaceutical sales (prescription and off-the counter) were estimated to be XAF 71.85 billion (or $147 million). Most of the drugs are procured and distributed to public health facilities through a procurement agency, L'Office Pharmaceutique National (L'OPN) that was established in 1995. The budget of L'OPN was XAF 1.166 billion (or $2.36 million) in 2010. This is a small percentage of the country's total pharmaceutical sales.

Gabon's pharmaceutical spending is not expected to grow dramatically over the short-term. That is because Gabon tends to have a higher incidence of communicable than noncommunicable diseases. Furthermore, a small percentage of the population is aged. A recent forecast estimated pharmaceutical sales to grow to about XAF 92.25 billion (or $169 million) by 2018. Annual per capita sales would be more or less constant—from $88 in 2013 to $90 by 2018. As a percentage of GDP they would also remain more or less constant—from 0.55 percent in 2013 to 0.5 percent in 2018 (BMI 2014). In addition, pharmaceutical sales represented about 24 percent of total health expenditures in 2013; they are expected to be 21 percent in 2018 (figure 3.16).

Figure 3.16 Pharmaceutical Sales, Historical Data and Forecasts, 2010–18

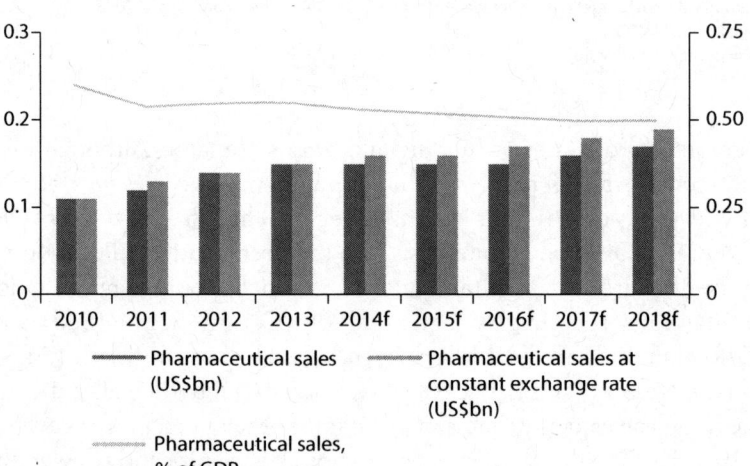

Pharmaceutical sales (US$bn)   Pharmaceutical sales at constant exchange rate (US$bn)

Pharmaceutical sales, % of GDP

Source: Business Monitor International—Gabon Pharmaceuticals and Healthcare Report Quarter 2. 2014.
Note: GDP = gross domestic product.

Summary

Is Gabon's health spending sufficient?

> How much should my country spend on health, given our current epidemiological profile relative to our desired level of health status, considering the effectiveness of health inputs that would be purchased at existing prices, and taking account of the relative value and cost of other demands on social resources? (World Health Organization 2003)

When estimating a country's health spending needs, several factors have to be considered: what are the existing epidemiological conditions, what are the social aspirations, what is the situation on technical and allocative efficiency of health inputs, what are existing prices, and what are alternative social uses of funds? Until the situation is not understood comprehensively, it is difficult to understand how much should Gabon spend on health. The Commission on Macroeconomics and Health quoted a figure of US$34 per capita as the minimum required for providing basic curative services to reach health-related MDGs in low-income countries (2001). The Taskforce on Innovative International Financing quoted a figure of US$44 per capita to strengthen health systems as well as provide essential health services in 49 low-income countries in 2009. The amount would go up to US$60 per capita by 2015 (Taskforce on Innovative International Financing for Health Systems 2010). This book only initiates this diagnostics, but further work is required to fully understand the gravity of the situation. There are concerns about allocative inefficiency. Much of the public health resources in Gabon go for curative care. A significant share of the recurrent budget is allocated to hospitals. Primary health care receives one-sixth of the recurrent health budget in 2011, public health received one-eighth. It should be noted that even Organization for Economic Cooperation and Development (OECD), which has a higher burden of noncommunicable diseases, allocates an average of 40 percent of their budgets to hospitals (Frogner and Anderson 2006). To improve allocative efficiency Gabon may want to reconsider its budget planning and methodologies.

In absolute terms, Gabon spends more on health than the average African country. Its expenditure is closer to the average middle-income country. And yet, its health outcomes are poor. There is room for additional public resources for health; OOP is considered significant. There is also room for improving the efficiency of resource allocation, the organization of services, their delivery and management, and the effectiveness of care. Public resources could be better allocated to activities that yield greater value for the money. For example, moving health care out of the resource-intensive hospital sector to ambulatory care services merits consideration. Placing a greater emphasis on disease prevention and health promotion is another.

Notes

1. Purchasing power parity.

2. WHO.
   http://apps.who.int/nha/database/StandardReport.aspx?ID=REP_WEB_MINI_TEMPLATE_WEB_VERSION&COUNTRYKEY=84537. The information comes from a simulation run based on a 1993 survey. It remains to be seen whether households have better protection since the introduction of the social protection program for health. The Government of Gabon is considering a household (poverty or income-expenditure) survey for 2015 in conjunction with a poverty assessment and NHA exercise.

3. Gabon has recently produced a National Health Accounts. However, the country still simulates household costs because recent household survey data is not available.

4. In April 2001, African Union countries met in Abuja, Nigeria. They pledged to increase government funding for health to a minimum of 15 percent. They also urged donor countries to scale up their support. http://www.who.int/healthsystems/publications/abuja_report_aug_2011.pdf.

5. These include reimbursement from other private insurance schemes and out-of-pocket contributions.

6. These differences were positive (payment higher than expected amount) for one hospital and negative (payment lower than expected amount) for the other six hospitals. No verification of this issue could be made in the absence of detailed documentation.

7. The GPRSP (2006), which covered the period from 2006 to 2008, targeted a reversal in the downward trend of the main development indicators and a significant improvement in the population's living conditions. It was prepared using a consultative approach, based on broad participation by civil society and was results-oriented. The ultimate goal was to achieve the Millennium Development Goals (MDGs). It was structured around four strategic areas: (i) promoting strong, sustainable, high quality and pro-poor economic growth, (ii) significantly improving access to basic social services by the entire population, (iii) improving infrastructure, and (iv) promoting good governance. World Bank, Gabon Public Expenditure Review, 2012.

8. Ministry of Health 2011–15 Strategy.

9. According to facility staff, a general practitioner may earn a monthly salary of XAF 400,000 in public facilities compared to a general practitioner employed by Caisse Nationale de Sécurité Sociale (CNSS) who earns XAF 1.5 million. At the Lambarene CHR hospital, incentive payments amount to 19 percent of total expenditures and 72 percent of the hospital's own revenue.

10. Ibid.

11. Because existing policies and norms are not disseminated; local managers are often unaware of them.

12. This estimate is limited to the cost burden on the budget. It does not taken into account off-budget contributions, which, as pointed out earlier, are significant. They range between one-third to one-half of total hospital financing.

13. As some figures appear to be data errors, these conclusions need to be validated with data that's been verified.

14. These figures do not include spending for vertical programs (including human immunodeficiency virus/acquired immune deficiency syndrome [HIV/AIDS]) or centrally

procured drugs; the geographic distribution is not available for these programs and services.

15. OECD (2012), "Pharmaceutical expenditure", in *Health at a Glance: Europe 2012*, OECD Publishing. http://dx.doi.org/10.1787/9789264183896-55-en. In comparison, members of the European Union, which have a higher level of noncommunicable diseases and a higher share of the aged, reported their drug spending was $460 per capita on average. To put these figures in perspective, their populations tend to be older and they have a higher level of noncommunicable diseases. Drug spending was 1.6 percent of GDP; it ranged between 0.7 percent of GDP in Norway to 2.4 percent of GDP in Hungary. In 2010 health spending for pharmaceuticals was about 19 percent of the total for health.

CHAPTER 4

National Health Insurance Program

Introduction

This chapter focuses on the national health insurance program and its development. It contains information on the various schemes, the population registered and the challenges in coverage. It offers a perspective on sources of financing, trends in spending, and issues of financial sustainability. The information herein came from various sources, including Caisse Nationale d'Assurance Maladie et de Garantie Sociale (National Health Insurance and Social Security; CNAMGS), World Health Organization (WHO), and others.

Key Findings

- The impetus for CNAMGS was to bring various schemes under one umbrella agency. Nevertheless, the three schemes run independently from each other: there is no pooling of resources or cross subsidization.
- CNAMGS has earmarked resources for its funding. So far, about 45 percent (2012) of it comes from contributions from formal sector workers (civil servants and private sector); the other half (55 percent) comes from between general and earmarked taxes.
- CNAMGS claims to have registered about 45 percent of the population by 2012.
- One of the greatest challenges: how to cover informal sector workers under CNAMGS.
- As a share of total spending, CNAMGS administrative expenses are significant.
- On a per capita basis, claims spending has increased. Claims expenditures make up about one-half of CNAMGS's total spending. The provider-payment mechanism and its impact needs further review.
- No financial or sustainability analysis is in place for CNAMGS. Steps to ensure the financial sustainability of the program are critical to its success.

Historical Perspective

The Gabonese social security systems started in the 1970s; various agencies provided services to different population subgroups. In 1975, the CNSS (Caisse Nationale de Securité Sociale 1975) began; in 1983, it was followed by the CNGS (Caisse Nationale de Garantie Sociale 1983). The CNSS managed the private sector scheme; the CNGS managed the public sector scheme. Under the CNGS, civil servants had access to subsidized health services in public facilities. CNGS covered informal and self-employed workers as well as the poor; they were fully subsidized by the state's budget. In fact, however, informal sector workers had minimal coverage. Under the CNSS medical fund, workers in the private formal sector had access to health services in CNSS-contracted facilities. Employers contributed based on a rate of 4.1 percent of salaries. Despite being highly subsidized, the two insurance funds faced recurring deficits. Patients sought care outside of the public system which had deteriorated. Beneficiaries, who could afford it, also enrolled in private for-profit insurance systems that offered access to services in private facilities only.

In the 1990s a new law (law 3/91 dating back to march 26, 1991) committed to providing free health care services. The government subsidized health care at public facilities for many population subgroups. Although economic growth was positive in the 1980s, that changed and declined in the 1990s, especially during periods of recession which occurred between 1999 and 2002. Consequently, in 1995, the government imposed user fees or copayments for acute care at hospitals. Even so, the system failed to recover from recurrent deficits and deficiencies (Musango et al. 2010).[1]

From 2003 to 2004, economic growth improved; in the public sector, resources for health went up. In 2007, the former President of Gabon, Omar Bongo, supported a reform whose goal was to establish a national health insurance program under the CNAMGS (Caisse Nationale d'Assurance Maladie et de Garantie Sociale). The law was ratified in 2007 (Decret 00510/2008) and brought about a major funding. The Gabonese health system was reorganized under the National Health Insurance Program. The sickness fund (now the CNAMGS) was separated from the benefit fund which remained under the authority of the CNSS. Purchaser and provider functions were split: the CNAMGS, which purchased services, came under the Ministry of Economy. Providers came under the Ministry of Health and Public Hygiene (MOHPH), Autonomous, or under the private sector. Following this reform, CNAMGS had compensatory and noncompensatory schemes. Gradually, CNAMGS is taking over all health insurance schemes that were originally under CNSS and CNGS. In 2009, CNGS (which covered the poor and informal sector workers) was effectively dissolved; the poor (not informal sector workers) were enrolled in the CNAMGS-GEF Scheme. CNSS is transferring its health facility network to the MOHPH (table 4.1).

Table 4.1 Pricing Policy at Public Health Facilities

Year	Pricing policy	Sources of financing
1991	Free health care at public health facilities	General taxes
1995	User fees or copayments at public hospitals	General taxes and out-of-pocket
2007	NHIP law ratified	
2009	GEF coverage initiated under CNAMGS with copayments for public and private clinics, pharmacies, hospital	General and earmarked taxes and levies and out-of-pocket
2011	Additionally, civil servants coverage initiated under CNAMGS with copayments for public and private clinics, pharmacies and hospitals	Payroll taxes and out-of-pocket
2013	Additionally, formal private sector coverage initiated under CNAMGS with copayments at public and private clinics, pharmacies and hospitals	Payroll taxes and out-of-pocket

Source: World Bank.
Note: CNAMGS = Caisse Nationale d'Assurance Maladie et de Garantie Sociale; GEF = Gabonais Economiquement Faibles; NHIP = National Health Insurance Program.

The universal health insurance program is compulsory for some and voluntary for others. CNAMGS holds the funds for multiple independent schemes: under the scheme for the poor (Gabonais Economiquement Faibles or GEF) enrollment is automatic and noncompensatory, the scheme for civil servants and the scheme for formal private sector workers is compulsory and compensatory. There are no schemes for informal sector workers at this time, although there are plans to develop one. For now their enrollment is voluntary. To achieve universal insurance coverage, CNAMGS planned to absorb the low-income scheme (GEF) in 2009, the civil servants scheme in 2011, and the private sector scheme in 2013. All the schemes are now under one umbrella institution, CNAMGS; however, their resources are yet not pooled and there is little cross subsidization. Integration of these various schemes in one pool or cross subsidization will help improve risk. As of this date, no formal feasibility or financial sustainability analysis has occurred. Nevertheless, these studies could be beneficial in assessing the viability and sustainability of the national health insurance program.

Coverage

Although the government has committed to provide universal health insurance coverage on a uniform basis to all Gabonese, the transition to full universal coverage is ongoing. Significant effort has increased coverage; CNAMGS reports their coverage has reached about 679,000 (June 2013) or 45 percent of the population[2] (figure 4.1).

Figure 4.1 CNAMGS Registration of Beneficiaries by Schemes in Percent, 2008–12

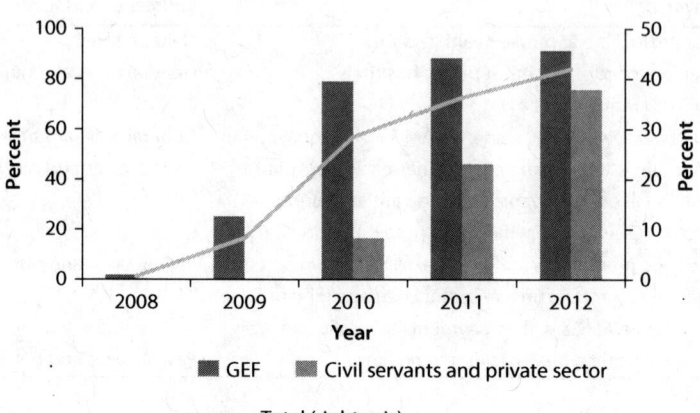

GEF ■ Civil servants and private sector

Total (right axis)

Source: CNAMGS, 2013, in WHO. July 2013. Health Financing in the African Region, Issue 17 (special issue), p. 17. http://www.aho.afro.who.int/sites/default/files/ahm/reports/631/ahm1705.pdf.
Note: GEF = Gabonais Economiquement Faibles.

- The scheme for the poor and the vulnerable population (Gabonais Economiquement Faibles, GEF) which began in 2008/09, is close to being a reality for this subgroup. An estimated 483,000 persons have coverage out of a target population of 490,000 (CNAMGS, 2013). Its beneficiaries were identified based on 2008 poverty assessment census, which used a proxy-means test. To be eligible for a health insurance subsidy, an adult must earn less than 80,000 Central Africa CFA Francs (XAF) a month ($160), which is equal to the monthly minimum wage in Gabon. A national census helped to elaborate on this list of beneficiaries. Means tests are themselves difficult to administer effectively; the current list reportedly contains errors and is likely to include wealthier quintiles. Challenges remain: namely how to ensure that the program captures the "economically deprived" on an annual basis. Since 2012, students attending public sector higher education are also covered under this scheme. Refugees are to be added in future.[3]
- The scheme for the civil servants, which began in 2011 has also achieved universal coverage of that sub-population (154,000). The scheme covers civil servants and their dependents.
- The scheme for formal private sector workers who were covered under Caisse Nationale De Securité Sociale (CNSS), came under the CNAMGS in 2013 (initial enrollment began in March 2013; small and medium size enterprises in September 2013). Coverage has reached about 40,000 persons (25 percent coverage of its target audience) (CNAMGS 2013). Coverage of formal private sector workers faces this challenge: many of its beneficiaries are covered under private insurance programs. The system could also suffer from adverse

---

Box 4.1 CNAMGS Electronic Registration Cards

The e-cards include information on "civil data and a photograph of the holder; two digitized fingerprints within the microprocessor ensure encryption and protection of the data. The multiapplication Java Card OS supports the opening and upgrading of software applications. The health insurance card is used in hospitals, pharmacies, and clinics to verify social security eligibility whilst protecting the confidentiality of personal data. Checks are performed using terminals with fingerprint sensors."

Source: Gemalto. The Gabon Health Program. www.gemalto.com.

---

selection. Coverage although compulsory, is not enforced. Because these households have other options under private health insurance, there may be little faith in the public delivery system.
- There are plans to consider enrolling informal sector workers and their families in an independent scheme under CNAMGS. These workers constitute a sizable portion of the population. Among the challenges: how to identify informal sector workers and develop the appropriate incentives to reduce adverse selection.

E-health. CNAMGS has a computerized system for registering beneficiaries.[4] CNAMGS has contracted *Gemalto* to launch CNAMGS registration cards (e-cards) electronically, beginning with GEF beneficiaries. CNAMGS has also launched a hotline for beneficiaries to access information about the location of accredited service providers. The country has at least 60 percent of its population using cellphones; however, in 2007, the proportion of the population using the Internet was less than 10 percent. Infrastructure and connectivity remain a concern (box 4.1).

Benefits Package

All beneficiaries of CNAMGS schemes have the same benefits package. The CNAMGS provides a comprehensive benefits package that has a list of included and excluded services. Their package complements the package of services and commodities financed under the MOHPH and other external financiers. The CNAMGS package of services favors clinical care, while MOHPH's package favors preventive and public health programs. CNAMGS promotes the use of generics (or brand name drugs if a generic not available), and the use of medicines from the national essential medicine list.[5] There is, however, a list of excluded medicines as well as a list of covered drugs. In addition, the GEF beneficiaries are also eligible for some nontraditional health benefits, such as a childbirth bonus and education costs for children under 18 years (box 4.2).

Box 4.2 CNAMGS Benefits Package

What's Included: Ambulatory services (medical consultations, nursing services, dental services, diagnostic tests, small surgeries, prenatal care, and postnatal care), hospitalizations (professional fees, room & board, drugs, and every service that is medically necessary, referrals, deliveries, diagnostic tests), drugs and devices, and foreign referrals (for cases that are curable but the service is not available in Gabon).

What's Excluded: antiretroviral therapy (ART), aesthetic surgery, traditional medicine, family planning commodities, screening (for example pap smear, mammogram, and others). Health promotion, prevention, and most public health services are excluded, as well as diseases funded directly by MOHPH under its vertical programs.

Prior authorization required: for certain diagnostic tests by a private provider, devices, and implants (especially corrective ones, and glasses), and referrals to other countries. Medical evacuation is covered but it also requires prior authorization. This generally covers catastrophic illnesses. The drug list includes those on the MOHPH's essential drug lists and some others. *Additional nonhealth benefits:* childbirth bonus and education costs for children under 18. These apply to for GEF beneficiaries only.

Source: CNAMGS website: http://itemcpclab.pro/cnamgs/la-cnamgs/le-panier-de-soins-de-la-cnamgs.

Purchasing of Services

CNAMGS has a mandate to provide public funds for both public and private health care. CNAMGS purchases services covered by its benefits package from accredited public and private health providers, clinics, hospitals, and selected drugs from accredited pharmacies. It contracts with public and private providers; these agreements help expand its network of services and provide more choices to its beneficiaries. However, public sector health facilities have received a blanket accreditation. In time, after satisfying certain standards, public sector facilities may be required to be accredited. In contrast, private sector health facilities must be accredited to belong to the CNAMGS network. A significant proportion of health facilities are accredited: 92 percent of public facilities, 80 percent of private facilities in Libreville, and 40 percent of private facilities outside Libreville (CNAMGS, 2013). There is a long waiting list for accreditation; many providers may not meet the minimum standards. Several private pharmacies have been accredited in Libreville, but that's not the case in rural areas. These facilities are unable to meet the basic requirements because a pharmacist is unavailable. Through the use of public funds, CNAMGS has the potential to bring a wider set of providers to serve the public program, but rural areas remain a challenge.

Payment Mechanism and Verification

CNAMGS uses a prospective fee-for-service payment mechanism. All facilities (clinics, pharmacies, and hospitals) follow a fee for service payment mechanism for

Table 4.2 Provider Payment Mechanisms by Type of Health Services

	Type of health services		
	Outpatient	Inpatient	Drugs
Public sector health facilities			
Pharmacies	n.a.	n.a.	Reimbursement is 80% of tariff for approved drugs
Medical centers	Reimbursement is 80% of the PHC tariff, 20% is copay by CNAMGS beneficiaries	n.a.	n.a.
Hospitals	Reimbursement is 80% of the Hospital tariff, 20% is copay by CNAMGS beneficiaries; noninsured beneficiaries pay 100% user fees	Reimbursement is 90% of Hospital tariff, 10% is copay by CNAMGS beneficiaries; noninsured beneficiaries pay 100% user fees	Reimbursement is 80% of tariff for approved drugs, 20% is copay by CNAMGS beneficiaries; noninsured beneficiaries pay 100% user fees
Parapublic health facilities			
CNSS (will be merged as part of the public sector)	Reimbursement is 80% of the Hospital tariff, 20% is copay by CNSS beneficiaries; noninsured beneficiaries pay 100% of user fees	Reimbursement on 90% of Hospital tariff, 10% is copay by CNSS beneficiaries; noninsured beneficiaries pay 100% of user fees	Reimbursement is 80% of tariff for approved drugs, 20% is copay by CNSS beneficiaries; noninsured beneficiaries pay 100% of user fees
Defense	n.a.	n.a.	n.a.
Private sector health facilities			
Pharmacies (contracted)	n.a.	n.a.	Reimbursement is 80% of CNAMGS agreed prices. Balance billing.
Clinics (contracted)	Reimbursement is 80% of CNAMGS agreed prices. Balance billing.	n.a.	n.a.
Hospitals (contracted)	Reimbursement is 80% of the CNAMGS contract price. Balance billing. Noninsured beneficiaries pay 100% as user fees.	Reimbursement is 90% of the CNAMGS contract price. Balance billing. Noninsured beneficiaries pay 100% as user fees.	Reimbursement is 80% of the CNAMGS contract price. Balance billing. Noninsured beneficiaries pay 100% as user fees.
Noncontracted facilities	100% user fees	100% user fees	100% user fees

Source: World Bank.

Note: CNAMGS = Caisse Nationale d'Assurance Maladie et de Garantie Sociale; CNSS = Caisse Nationale de Securité Sociale; PHC = primary health care; n.a. = not applicable.

outpatient and inpatient services. CNAMGS has standardized its prices by type of service for all providers. However, prices for the same service may differ depending on the location and between public and private facilities. Hospital fees are higher than clinics. For example, a general consultation at a clinic could cost XAF 3,000 and at a hospital it could cost XAF 5,000 (2012). Different specialists have different rates: a specialist consultation could cost XAF 8,000, a normal delivery XAF 40,000 (2012).[6] While public sector health providers receive their salaries through budget, private sector health providers rely on reimbursement and OOP. Reimbursement rates therefore also vary by public and private facilities.

Copayments came about to reduce moral hazard at all public and private facilities. Copayments are 20 percent for public facilities for ambulatory care and 10 percent for a chronic long-term illness. Covered pharmaceuticals also require a 20 percent copayment. Deliveries/childbirth expenditures are fully subsidized by the government. All patients are subject to these copays. GEF beneficiaries may be exempt, but they require special permission first.[7] The private sector has balance billing.[8] Although contracted rates are fixed, patient contributions (copays) could be higher. Copays create obstacles to the use of services, especially for the poor (table 4.2).

The fee-for-service type of payment mechanism offers an incentive for services based on quantity and supplier induced demand. For example, recent data shows that C-sections, which have a higher reimbursement, have doubled in the past 10-years from 5 percent in 2001 to 10 percent in 2012 (GDHS 2013). The impact that fee for service payments have on the cost and use of benefits needs further study. There is also an opportunity to offering incentives to improve the quality of care.

Reimbursement occurs after the service is rendered and subject to claims processing. CNAMGS reimburses accredited providers for outpatient and inpatient services and accredited pharmacies for drugs. CNAMGS also has an ad hoc claims audit process. The payment system is manual; manual claims handling results in delays in reimbursement as well as other inefficiencies.

Sources of Financing

CNAMGS has mixed sources of financing, including general and earmarked taxes and social security contributions (employer-employee contributions). Financing is mostly progressive. However, financing is not pooled in one pot; rather it is separate for each subset of the population.

The GEF program is financed through taxes and is not expected to be self-sufficient. The GEF is financed through general (12 percent of the GEF fund), earmarked and indirect taxes (88 percent of the GEF fund). The latter comes from a 10 percent levy on mobile phone company revenues; these make up 80 percent of earmarked and indirect taxes,[9] and a 1.5 percent levy on money transfers outside the CEMAC (the economic community of Central African states); they make up 20 percent of the earmarked and indirect taxes.[10] Most of those identified as GEF beneficiaries are the poor whose individual adult monthly income is below XAF 80,000 [Decret 0023/2007 and Decret 0051/2008]; they are covered by earmarked and indirect taxes. Students and other vulnerable groups are covered by general taxes. Between 2008 and 2011, revenue from earmarked taxes doubled; revenue from general taxes stayed the same in 2011 and made up about 12 percent of total revenue of the GEF fund that year. Releases from the treasury and tax departments are reportedly delayed. These delays affect the credibility of the funds, particularly for the poor and for civil servants. GEF's financing has been criticized for being narrow, unsustainable, and vulnerable to economic shocks (table 4.3).

On the other hand, the schemes for civil servants and formal private sector workers have built-in contributions and are self-sufficient. For civil servants, the employer contributes about 4.1 percent of taxable wages, the employee pays 2.5 percent of taxable wages; the retiree contribution is 1.5 percent of his or her pension. Contributions received from employers and employees under the civil servants scheme are almost as much as those received from earmarked taxes

Table 4.3 CNAMGS, Funding of the Main Insurance Schemes

	Beneficiary groups			
	Civil servants and public agents	Private and par-apublic sector	GEF (poor and vulnerable)	Informal/independent
Membership	Compulsory	Compulsory	Automatic	Voluntary
Target population	154,000	150,000	490,000	722,000
(Percent of total population)	(10%)	(10%)	(32%)	(48%)
Waiting period before registration is confirmed	2 months	2 months	immediate	To be defined
Employer contribution (percent of wage)	4.1% (state contribution)	4.1%	0	0
Employee/worker's contribution (percent of wage)	2.5%	2.5%	0	To de defined
Other sources	Investment income and fines	Investment income and fines	10% tax on mobile phones; 1.5% tax on foreign transfers; Budget contribution of XAF 25,000 or US$50 per registered person	
Per capita (average) premium contributions in XAF and US$ (2011)	XAF 113,000, US$234	XAF 113,000, US$234	XAF 40,000, US$84	n/a
Copayment (percent of service user fees)	20% (10% for long-term chronic diseases)	20% (10% for long-term chronic diseases)	20% (10% for long-term chronic diseases)	To be defined

Source: CNAMGS documentation and interviews.
Note: XAF = Central Africa CFA Francs.

Figure 4.2 CNAMGS, Sources of Financing—GEF and Civil Servant Schemes, 2008–12

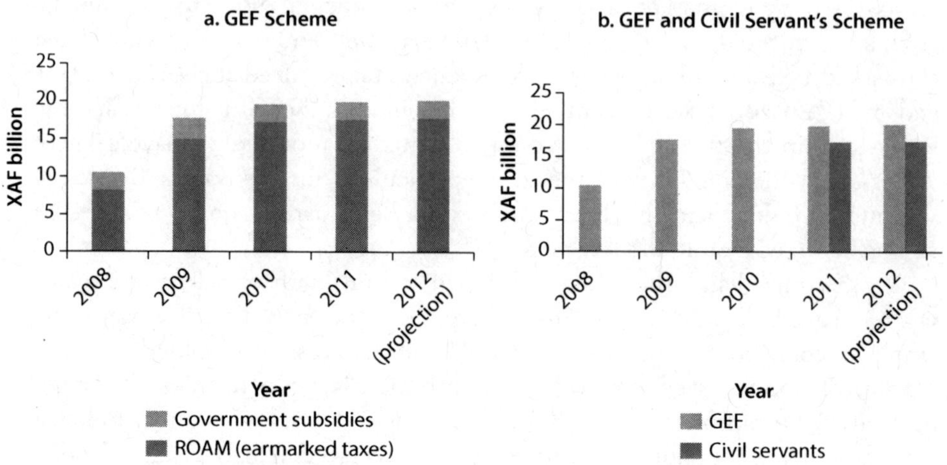

a. GEF Scheme

b. GEF and Civil Servant's Scheme

Legend (a): Government subsidies / ROAM (earmarked taxes)

Legend (b): GEF / Civil servants

Source: Inoua and Musango 2013.
Note: GEF = Gabonais Economiquement Faibles; ROAM = Redevance Obligatoire à l'Assurance Maladie.

under the GEF Scheme. For formal private sector workers, the employer and employee contributions are the same as those in the civil servants program. On average, the formal sector contribution comes to about XAF 113,000 (or $234) per registered person per year (figure 4.2).

Spending Patterns

The CNAMGS consumes a significant amount of resources. In 2012 per capita spending for registered beneficiaries in the CNAMGS program was XAF 37,000 (or $69). That same year, operating costs represented 40 percent of CNAMGS's total health spending per capita.[11] As registration increases, per capita spending for operations is expected to decline (figure 4.3).

Claims spending has gone up over time. The fee-for-service payment mechanism is likely to lead to cost escalation around claims. In 2012, claims made up 60 percent of CNAMGS's total expenditures for all schemes. That figure doubled from the previous year. On a per capita basis, annual claims spending have increased significantly over the years; in 2012, it reached XAF 22,000 (or $41) (figure 4.4).

Providers consider claims reimbursement essential for operating health facilities. They retain most of their earnings for this purpose. Given the fee for service payment mechanism, claims could increase at a far greater pace than revenue is generated. However, more data is required to assess this situation. Four years of claims data show significant growth. A claims breakdown does not exist at this time; understanding what drives costs is critical however and warrants further investigation. In Ghana, for example, drugs consumed a significant portion of claims (55 percent in 2011).[12] Other countries have used gatekeeping or

Figure 4.3 CNAMGS Program Total Per Capita Spending, 2009–12

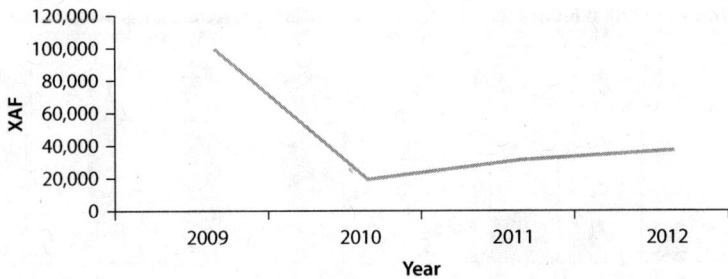

Source: World Bank's estimates using CNAMGS income-expenditure data based on the WHO report.
Note: family benefits provided under the CNAMGS benefit package are excluded from this estimate.

Figure 4.4 CNAMGS's Annual Claims Spending Per Capita, XAF, 2009–12

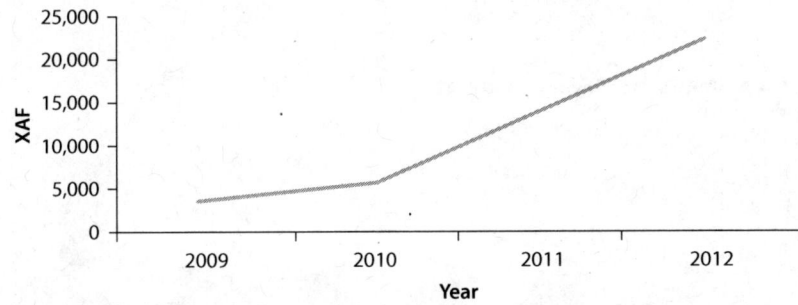

Source: World Bank's estimates using CNAMGS income-expenditure data based on a WHO report.

reimbursement ceilings to control these costs. An assessment of the current system is warranted; a more efficient system might help control costs. Measuring the impact of the current program on the health and welfare of its beneficiaries is also a good idea (figure 4.5).

Family services are included within the package for GEF beneficiaries. One-fourth of claims expenditures are for family benefits (including the childbirth bonus and schooling costs for children under 18 years). These family benefits are not traditionally a part of health insurance programs in other countries. Spending for these services, which include a family allowance and maternal health care, rose from XAF 1.3 billion in 2008 to XAF 9.5 billion in 2011. Spending on general health-care coverage for the poor jumped from XAF 447 million in 2009 to XAF 6.3 billion in 2011.[13] In 2011, family services represented at least 60 percent of total GEF beneficiary benefits—excluding administrative costs.

Administrative costs are significant. Operating costs are also significant. In 2012 they represented about 30–40 percent of total expenditures after excluding family benefits provided under CNAMGS. Other countries that are similar have operating costs of around 10 percent.

Figure 4.5 CNAMGS Expenditures, 2008–12

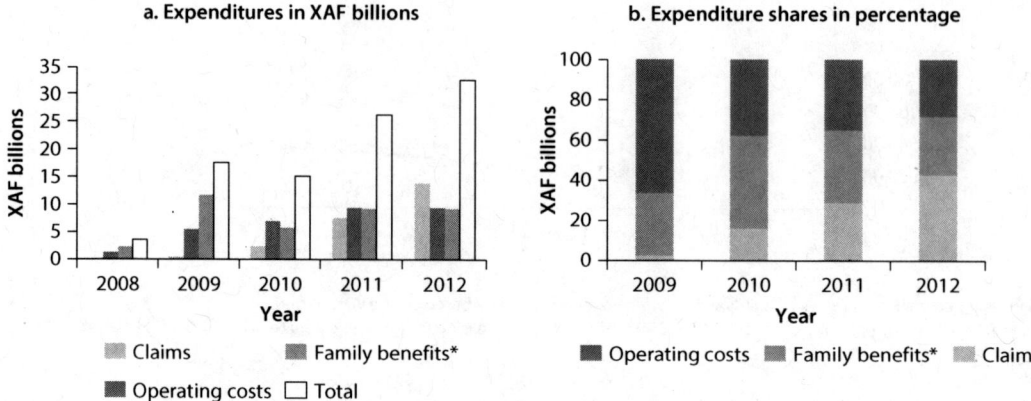

a. Expenditures in XAF billions

b. Expenditure shares in percentage

Claims Family benefits*

Operating costs Total

Operating costs Family benefits* Claims

Source: CNAMGS, 2013, in Source: WHO. July 2013. Health Financing in the African Region, Issue 17 (special issue), p. 17.
http://www.aho.afro.who.int/sites/default/files/ahm/reports/631/ahm1705.pdf.

Figure 4.6 CNAMGS, Net Savings, 2008–12

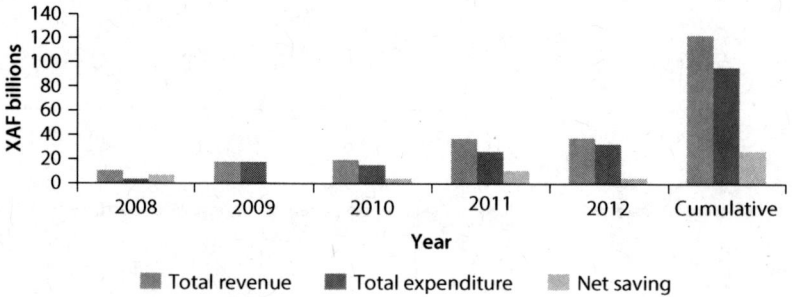

Total revenue Total expenditure Net saving

Source: World Bank's estimates based on CNAMGS income-expenditure data according to a WHO report.
Note: XAF = Central Africa CFA Francs.

Reserves or Net Savings

In the absence of an actuarial analysis, this book estimated the income-expenditure data reported by CNAMGS. Resources under CNAMGS's various schemes are not pooled and it is difficult to determine how much CNAMGS has in its reserves. Its reserves policy is not clear. Based on available information for income and expenditures, it appears that thus far CNAMGS has accumulated a reserve of XAF 27 billion or 22 percent of the total fund (2008–12). This is a significant reserve. It suggests there are sufficient reserves to cover more than 12 months (12–18 months) of claims based on a 2012 claims estimate and after adjusting for inflation. Actuaries often recommend that reserves for a more mature health insurance program should have funds amounting to about four to six months of anticipated claims. A more thorough actuarial analysis would more accurately reveal what is in this reserve fund and it might offer some policy suggestions on the amounts that should be in reserve (figure 4.6).

What Has the NHIP Reform Achieved?

The following analysis lists pre-2008 national health service (NHS) concerns and the government's response, which led to the NHIP. It also discusses the NHIP's achievements and challenges.

First, given the volatility of the health budget, including low releases over the past decade, a national health insurance fund was created to provide multiyear access to funds for health and to provide it with flexibility. Taxes were earmarked and allocated to the fund for this purpose. In addition, the fund was able to collect its own contributions. Together, earmarked taxes and contributions were regarded as more progressive; the better off contributed more than those who were not. Earmarked funds provided subsidies for the poor. In this way, NHIP received 27 percent of public funds. Public financing of total health spending increased from 40 percent in 2008 to 51 percent in 2012 (NHA 2013). In 2012, private contributions from employers and employees represented one-half of NHIP funds.

Second, many Gabonese believe that the public sector suffers from a culture of limited accountability. To keep track and control of resources, the fund holder, CNAMGS, is a third party agency, under the Ministry of Economy. The roles of payer/purchaser and provider have been separated to ensure better accountability.

Third, pre-2008 health facility access, especially in rural areas, was limited. To broaden access to health facilities, the NHIP was mandated to use public monies to purchase services from the public and nonpublic sectors. However, it is not clear if private sector participation has been beneficial and if so, for whom. The private sector is not active in rural areas. Furthermore, the poor tends not to use it because it is not generally available and because of balance billing practices.

Fourth, pre-2008 there was low utilization of health services, poor performance, and poor quality of care. In Gabon, budget preparation and the release process has been historical and incremental. It does not create an incentive for improved performance, productivity, or accountability. Changing budget procedures is solely the responsibility of the Ministry of Budget. Incentives could be set up within the budgetary process, but the sector decided to use a provider payment mechanism to get appropriate reactions and create incentives to help increase the use of health services (table 4.4).

Fifth, the discussion on demand-side financing suggested the possibility of a more targeted way to protect the vulnerable. Money would follow to beneficiaries, not the other way around. The health care system would be aligned with the demands of the population with appropriate emphasis on the vulnerable. Health systems would be strengthened in areas where the vulnerable lived and for services that they most needed.

What has demand-side financing achieved and has it resulted in the government meeting program objectives and targets? As a consequence of the NHIP, findings show (i) more reliable financing as well as multiyear reserve funds. Reliability can improve once funds under the various schemes are pooled. Financing is more progressive since most of it derives from general taxes,

Table 4.4 Accountability Mechanisms Set Up in the NHIP

Structural changes	Actual NHIP, 2013
Accountability mechanisms	Separation of payer and provider
	Contractual agreements between NHIS/payer and providers (public, mission, for-profit)
	Ex post reimbursement based on outputs
	Mandatory reporting, and reimbursement based on reporting
Expanding access to services	Accreditation and contractual agreements between payer and provider to serve certain areas, and certain beneficiaries
	Can do selective contracting

Source: World Bank.
Note: NHIP is National Health Insurance Program.

progressive earmarked taxes, and payroll taxes; (ii) a concerted effort to target the vulnerable and the poor and to finance their health care; (iii) an effort to streamline service standards (through accreditation) and to develop accountability of providers. Providers are contracted and reimbursed based on the services they render. Or they are accountable to provide data on their services; and (iv) there is an increased network of providers because services are purchased from public and private providers. In Gabon, some accredited providers come from the nonpublic sector. This feature has helped improve access to services. Because provider payment mechanisms are based on output, the NHIP also has an opportunity to motivate provider and consumer behaviors and to set pricing controls.

Positive results include the following: (i) The out-of-pocket share of total health spending has declined. Before 2009, the health financing situation in Gabon suggested that out-of-pocket spending remained significant (in the range of 50 percent or more between 1995 and 2008). However, in 2012, the out-of-pocket spending share declined to about 41 percent of total health spending in 2012 (NHA 2013). (ii) Health service use by the insured (of all economic backgrounds) has been significantly better than that of the uninsured (of all economic backgrounds). Clearly, if free health care is offered, it will lead to improved utilization among all economic groups. The use of health services has increased among all economic groups, including the poor and the nonpoor (who can afford care). However, there are implications of moral hazard and supplier-induced demand. (iii) A more recent survey does not exist to corroborate the effect the NHIP has had on household financial protection.

However, some adverse post-NHIP effects include the following. (i) Many people, including the near poor (those who work in the informal sector), do not have access to the NHIP. There are no schemes targeting informal sector workers and their families. (ii) Many people, including the poor, do not have access to affordable health care; copayments are still required. This may be a factor in their low utilization of health services. According to a household survey (GDHS 2013), the population using health services was skewed toward the nonpoor. Many of the poor (who are insured under the CNAMGS claims universal health insurance coverage) continued to use health services less often relative to the nonpoor). Despite all the benefits offered under the NHIP, CNAMGS's overall coverage remains stagnant at close to 45 percent of the population.

The questions that remain unanswered and need critical attention are: How long will it take the government to scale-up coverage under the NHIP? Will there be sufficient funds, risk pooling, and administrative support to meet the 2015 millennium development goal (MDG) targets? If the disparity in coverage is not a priority, then Gabon is likely to continue to underperform when it comes to health outcomes.

Summary

The scheme for informal sector workers, who make up about one-half of the population and were originally covered under CNGS, is to be established as a voluntary scheme at some future time. Should this Scheme be voluntary or mandatory? National health insurance programs throughout the world have struggled to cover informal sector workers. The decision ultimately rests on whether this population subgroup should be subsidized by the government and where the resources would come from. Such discussions have yet to take place in Gabon's public forums.

CNAMGS covers about 45 percent of the population (2012). To reach its target for universal health insurance, further action is necessary. A first step would be to conduct an actuarial analysis to ensure the financial sustainability of the fund. The benefit package is comprehensive, including nonhealth benefits for GEF beneficiaries, but premiums are not actuarially based. Should the non-health benefits be part of the health insurance scheme? Second, the program remains fragmented; each scheme operates independently when they could benefit from a pooling of resources, cross-subsidization and reduced administrative costs. Can pooling be considered? Third, often releases from treasury and the tax departments are delayed. These delays affect the credibility of the funds, particularly the GEF (for the poor) and for civil servants. Can an early dialogue be led between CNAMGS and the treasury to ensure a more efficient and sustainable flow of funds?

Over time expenditures have grown. Claims (for services and medicines) have almost doubled in two years; in 2012, they represented 60 percent of CNAMGS's expenditures. Because of the fee for service provider payment mechanism, claims could increase at a far greater pace than the generation of revenue generation. However, additional data and an actuarial analysis are necessary to assess the claims situation and to determine whether a more efficient system could be proposed. Some of the cost controls used in other countries includes gatekeeping and reimbursement ceilings. These measures however require that the quality of care at first level health facilities is adequate. Whether these might work in Gabon and the impact they might have on program beneficiaries requires further study. Administration costs are also a significant share of expenditures (30–40 percent of CNAMGS expenditures in 2012). This is much higher than in other countries (some examples include, the Philippines and Ghana) that have pooled schemes. Further analysis may reveal whether Gabon's administrative costs are a result of fragmented schemes and multiple administrative functions.

Notes

1. http://www.aho.afro.who.int/en/ahm/issue/17/reports/la-caisse-nationaled %E2%80%99assurance-maladie-et-de-garantie-sociale-du-gabon-un.

2. The population is estimated to include about 1.2 million citizens and another 0.3 million residents.

3. Although many countries, such as the Russian Federation and the United Arab Emirates, are reducing government subsidies to noncitizens Gabon has taken steps to be inclusive. Gabon intends to improve the quality of health for all those who live in the country.

4. Oxford Business Group. 2012. The Report: Gabon 2011. http://books.google.com/books?id=qm8900AFGfoC&pg=PA105&lpg=PA105&dq=gabon+cnamgs&source=bl&ots=_zb0jdBUnf&sig=-A1wyORjlPyVUK5qNKblosqKklU&hl=en&sa=X&ei=Mx S2UeeMDtOt4AOetoD4BQ&ved=0CGkQ6AEwCw#v=onepage&q=gabon%20 cnamgs&f=false.

5. CNAMGS website—http://itemcpclab.pro/cnamgs/la-cnamgs/le-panier-de-soins-de-la-cnamgs/. CNAMGS Arrete 0021/MTEPS/MSHP—http://itemcpclab.pro/cnamgs/wp-content/uploads/2012/04/Arrêté-0021-panier-soins-signé.pdf.

6. http://itemcpclab.pro/cnamgs/wp-content/uploads/2012/05/Directives-DG.pdf.

7. The government directive N0022/PR/2007 Article 64 says: "the insured participates, unless exempted by a circular from the Ministry of Health and Ministry of Social Security, in the payment of services through the principle of copayment as fixed by decree."

8. Balance billing, sometimes also called extra billing, is the practice of a *healthcare provider* billing a *patient* for the difference between what the patient's *health insurance* chooses to reimburse and what the provider chooses to charge. http://en.wikipedia.org/wiki/Balance_billing.

9. The Social Guarantee Fund is funded by an indirect tax called the Mandatory Health Insurance Fee (Redevance Obligatoire à l'Assurance Maladie, ROAM), Ordonnance 0022/2007.

10. The levies are collectively called the *redevance obligatoire à l'assurance maladie* (ROAM) or mandatory health insurance levy.

11. Per capita health spending is based on the entire population of Gabon. The estimate per capita CNAMGS spending is based exclusively on beneficiaries registered under CNAMGS.

12. Saleh, Karima. 2012. The Health Sector in Ghana: A comprehensive assessment. Directions in Development. World Bank. Washington, D.C.

13. http://www.who.int/bulletin/volumes/91/5/13-020513/en.

CHAPTER 5

Assessing Costs and Options for Bridging the Coverage Gaps

Introduction

The chapter briefly assesses what additional resources may be needed by Gabon in the medium term as it embarks on its goal for universal health insurance coverage. The book recommends that the government consider a comprehensive costing exercise to understand their financial obligations to meet universal coverage targets in the medium term, and to assess what additional resources are required and where those resources will be sought from. The chapter attempts to review the fiscal situation that would allow resources for health in the medium term. Fiscal space is defined as "the budgetary room to increase government spending—for a given sector without impairing fiscal solvency, that is, the government's ability to cover its expenditure and service its debt." The chapter estimates the costs for expanding insurance coverage according to different scenarios, and based on these costs, explores several options for bridging the gaps.[1]

Key Findings

- There is a need for additional public resources to cover the remaining population and meet the goal to expand coverage under Caisse Nationale d´Assurance Maladie et de Garantie Sociale (National Health Insurance and Social Security; CNAMGS).
- Economic growth is likely to inject additional funds to the health sector. However, since economic growth has slowed, the growth in resources for health is conservative.
- Prioritization of the budget for health and an improved execution of the budget are likely to inject additional resources for health. Nevertheless, additional resources will likely depend on reprioritizing and a more efficient and effective execution of the budget.

- With earmarked and indirect taxes as well as contributions from employers and employees, the country has injected additional funds for health in the CNAMGS program. Although some of this could be sustained, additional resources are unlikely. The challenge going forward is that the population subgroup of informal sector workers are unlikely to be in a position to make a financial contribution.
- New earmarked taxes are unlikely to be introduced or to be increased as a new source of revenue for Gabon's health sector. The political window for the introduction of new taxes has to be considered.
- There are two areas by which external financing could be injected into the health sector. The first is Official Development Assistance. However, the prospect is not good for two reasons: traditionally, the amount is low and Gabon is an upper-middle-income country (UMIC). Borrowing and increasing debt for health could be an option. Whether the government would be willing to reopen its debt to increase government spending—particularly for health—is uncertain.
- Finally, large gains in efficiency could be realized. World Health Organization (WHO) notes that in general 20–40 percent of spending on health is wasted because of such inefficiencies. There are areas that could be considered for cost controls, improved allocative efficiency, and investment in interventions that could result in greater value for the money (for example, primary health care).

Costing the CNAMGS Expansion of Coverage

Gabon's goal, an ambitious one, is to attain universal health insurance coverage, and cover the entire population under the national health insurance program (NHIP) in the medium term. Current enrollment is at 45 percent (2012). One-half of the formal sector is covered; 90 percent of the targeted poor are enrolled. The informal sector is not insured. To estimate the financing needed to expand coverage to the remaining population, three scenarios have been established. The assumptions are: by 2018, about 74 percent of the population will be covered under CNAMGS, and the premium rates are inflationary adjusted over the years (figure 5.1).

- Scenario 1, envisages that the government will fully subsidize the enrollment of the poor (Gabonais Economiquement Faibles [GEF] beneficiaries) and the informal sector.
- Scenario 2 envisages that the government will fully subsidize the enrollment of the poor (GEF beneficiaries) and partially (50 percent) subsidize the informal sector.
- Scenario 3 envisages that the government will fully subsidize the enrollment of the poor (GEF beneficiaries) but will not offer any subsidy to the informal sector.

Figure 5.1 Costing of CNAMGS Coverage Expansion in XAF

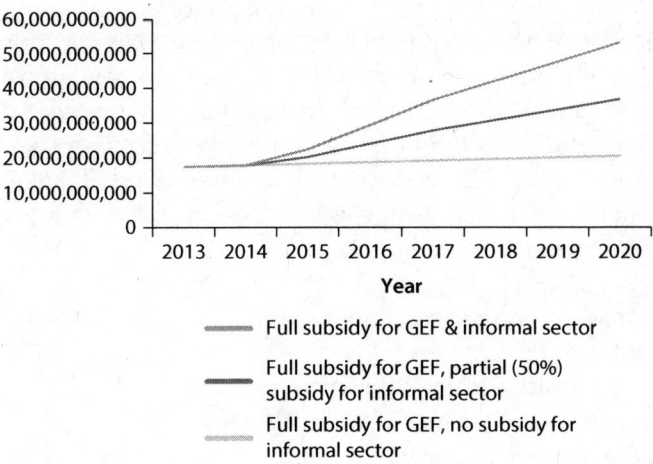

Source: World Bank's estimates.
Note: GEF = Gabonais Economiquement Faibles.

The simulation suggests that CNAMGS will need financing that would be between XAF 21–43 billion by 2018 just for the coverage of GEF (100 percent coverage) and informal sector (74 percent) beneficiaries. This amount is estimated to be around 15 percent (if informal sector is not subsidized) to 42 percent (if informal sector is fully subsidized) of government health spending (GHS) by 2018. The latter will be about 0.3 percent of gross domestic product (GDP) by 2018. This suggests that GHS as share of GDP should increase from 1.7 percent of GDP in 2012 to at least 2 percent of GDP by 2018. We have not taken into consideration other investments that may be required for reform of CNAMGS, such as claims management. We also have not estimated the investments for primary health care and public health programs. See appendix B1.

Given the challenges faced internationally on coverage of informal sector under NHIP, CNAMGS will have to consider various models with either full or partial subsidies incentivizing the enrollment of informal sector workers within CNAMGS. Unless an appropriate incentive is introduced and financing secured, it is less likely that this coverage level will be seen by 2018.

Defining Fiscal Space for Health

Heller (2006) defines fiscal space as "the budgetary room to increase government spending for a given sector without impairing fiscal solvency, i.e. the government's ability to cover its expenditure and service its debt." Estimating the fiscal space for health in a given country means looking at possible options (such as policy instruments or fiscal factors) that could increase resources for health within a macroeconomic and fiscal context. They include options that do not necessarily modify the budget's share for health. Fiscal space does not necessarily imply an injection of additional public resources. Instead, it may result from the reprioritization of other sectors, re-allocation to cost-effective interventions and/or realizing substantial efficiency gains through reforms in service delivery (for example a change in focus to primary and preventive care; revision of provider payment systems). Within this general analytical framework, Tandon and Cashin (2010) recommend assessing fiscal space for health in five different ways that encompass revenues and expenditures:

- Favorable macroeconomic conditions that may translate into more resources for the state
- Reprioritizing health within government spending
- Generating additional earmarked resources for health
- Official development assistance for health
- Increase the efficiency of government health spending.

Favorable Macroeconomic Conditions

As the economy grows, so will resources for health. Growth in national income, if translated into more resources for the state, will automatically increase the nominal volume of health resources.

The elasticity of GHS as a result of growth in GDP averaged at about 1.7 between 1995 and 2012 (that is a 1 percent increase in GDP is likely to result in a 1.7 percent increase in GHS). However, when dissecting the situation, no clear trend in elasticity is noted pre-2009. Between 1995 and 2001 the growth in GHS as a result of the growth in GDP was about 3 percent. This has probably been the most positive period for GHS growth in the past 20 years. From 2009 to 2012, the elasticity of GHS as a result of the growth in GDP averaged about 1.8 percent. However, when dissecting this period, elasticity varied considerably by year: 2.4 (2010–11), and 0.8 (2011–12). The spurt in GHS was noted at the introduction of the CNAMGS in 2009.

According to International Monetary Fund (IMF) and World Development Indicators (WDI) estimates, economic growth rates are positive (averaging about 6 percent) in nominal terms between 2012 and 2018 (WDI 2013). A simulation was run for 2012–18, with three case scenarios for elasticity (0.8, 1.8, and 3.0). By 2018, GHS as share of GDP would range between 0.92 percent (that is decline as share of GDP if elasticity is 0.8) to 2.30 percent (that is increase as share of GDP if elasticity is 3). However, in real term GHS as share of GDP would range between 1.42 percent (if elasticity is 0.8) and 2.38 percent (if elasticity is 3) by 2018. In order for government to scale up coverage, especially of the informal sector, under the CNAMGS, additional resources are required, and elasticity of above 1.8 is necessary for GHS share of GDP to be around 2.3 percent (figure 5.2 and appendix B2).

Figure 5.2 Trends in Elasticity of Government Health Spending to GDP, 1995–2018

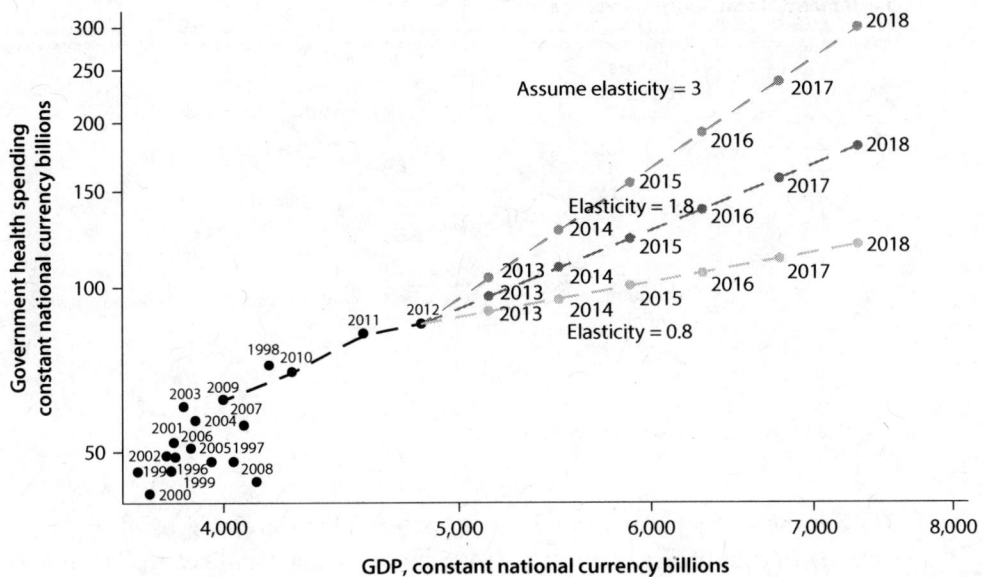

Source: World Bank.
Note: Elasticity is estimated as growth in GHS over growth in GDP; it explains the growth in GHS as GDP grows. GDP growth is based on an average of 6 percent during the simulation period (IMF). Actual data for 1995-2012. Simulated estimates for 2013-2018.

Reprioritizing Health within Government Spending

Another potential source of fiscal space for health is the reprioritization of health within the government budget. Looking at the budget's share for health can help determine if there is room for increasing government spending on health. As a reference point, UMIC devote an average of 6.2 percent of GDP to the health sector, and about 3.4 percent as share of GDP is from the public sector (WDI, 2013). While Gabon's public sector share to the health sector is only 1.7 percent of GDP. UMIC devote about 10-11 percent of their government spending to the health sector (WHO, 2010). In comparison to its peers, Gabon dedicates a small share of its government budget to health; in 2012, the share was 7.2 percent. Health is among the smallest allocations in Gabon's budget; housing is at one percent, social security at 2 percent; all of them are far behind education which is at 15 percent (figure 5.3).

General services represent almost 30 percent of government expenditures (average 2005–09). Actual expenditures are reported to be slightly less than the amounts budgeted for the health and social protection sectors. Between 2005 and 2009, on average, health expenditures accounted for 70–90 percent of the health budget. On the other hand, payment authorizations exceeded budgeted expenditures for education and general services (105 percent and 109 percent, respectively).

Figure 5.3 Budget Share by Sectors as Percentage of Government's Total Budget, Average for 2005–09

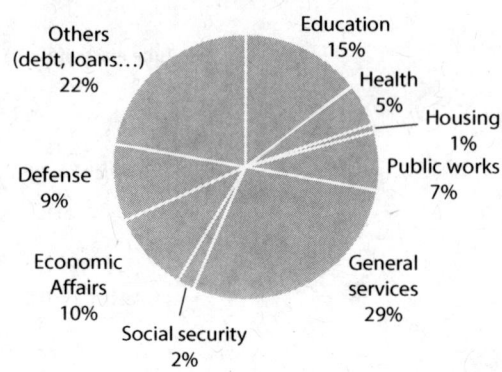

Source: Gabon Public Expenditure Review, World Bank, 2012b.

Given the budget structure, there is potential for increasing fiscal space for health by re-prioritizing sectors that favor human capital and health. Three possible scenarios offer realistic options.

- Scenario 1 is based on the assumption that the budget's share for health will remain at 2009 estimates, namely 5.5 percent of the budget.
- Scenario 2 is more optimistic. It assumes that GHS will represent 6.5 percent of the budget (based on a recent average).
- Scenario 3 assumes that GHS will increase to 8 percent.

The most recent estimates show that GHS is trending upward (similar to scenario 3). In 2012 GHS represented 7.2 percent of total government spending. The first two scenarios imply a decrease in the growth of real government spending on health through 2020, given recent increases above respective thresholds. The third scenario allows the generation of additional resources in real terms (compared to the 2009 status quo).

A different scenario will impact national income in a variety of ways. If 8 percent of the budget is dedicated to the health sector through 2020, government spending for health will go up slightly, from 1.7 percent (2012) to 2 percent of GDP (2020). This is consistent with the estimated cost for expanding NHIP coverage (see section on costing).

Although the government has taken steps to increase the health budget, it seems unlikely that the health and social sectors will become priorities for forthcoming public investments (a doubling of amounts—XAF 704 billion—compared to the previous year). In the latest budget estimates for 2013, the health sector represented only 7 percent of total investments; in comparison, public works, transport, and the extractive industry attracted the majority of budget subsidies. Taken together, those sectors absorbed 78 percent of the new planned investments; health and education accounted for 22 percent. The

Table 5.1 Public Investments in Priority Sectors, 2013 Budget

Sector	Amount	Relative increase (compared to 2012) (%)	Share to total public investments (%)
Public works, transports, extractive industry	XAF 499 billion	+91	70
Education	XAF 92 billion	+53	13
Oil, energy and hydraulic resources	XAF 59 billion	+270	8
Health	XAF 54 billion	+40	7

Source: World Bank calculation from Gabon's Ministry of Economy data.

feasibility of increasing the health budget will also depend on the country's budget practices. In the President's "Plan for Gabon emergent," human capital and social sectors are not given a high degree of priority; the focus is more on production sectors. Furthermore, Ministry of Health and Public Hygiene (MOHPH) has little say in the allocation and reallocation processes and it does not have an oversight role for CNAMGS's budget. It is unlikely that this will change during a preelection period (table 5.1).

The country is undergoing a reform to improve its budget preparation and execution. The goal is to boost the predictability of government expenditures by sector (Ministry of Planning 2009). It is anticipated that an improvement in budgetary discipline and accountability may benefit the health sector and reduce overspending. Improvements in budget execution can generate its own additional fiscal space for the sector (up to XAF 10,000 million as of 2009[2]). Since the introduction of CNAMGS, it is anticipated that joint budgeting will take place among the Ministries of Economy, Social Affairs, and Health for the purpose of defining annual allocations for CNAMGS. This would allow the state's budget to be more predictable and enable the administration of the CNAMGS to be more efficient. On a less positive note, the reform of budget policies may also reduce the government's margin of maneuverability. It could also increase the rigidity of budget-setting to the detriment of nonproductive sectors. In some instances, this rigidity has also aided in the expansion of progressive economic and social reforms (Cetrangolo 2010). However, fiscal rigidity can also have adverse effects (CDG 2007; World Bank 2007) on social and health sectors. Gabon will need to monitor this.

Generating Additional Earmarked Resources for Health

Fiscal space can come from raising revenues through taxes, mandatory contributions, and borrowing. Improving the collection of tax revenue is the first option for generating additional resources for the government. The introduction of new earmarked taxes, such as a sin (tobacco and/or alcohol) tax,[3] is another way to generate resources for the health sector. Borrowing is also possible.

In Gabon, government revenues have been stable over time at around 30 percent of GDP. Between 2004 and 2008, revenues, as a share of GDP, increased slightly following a boost in oil prices. Oil represents a third of government resources, mainly in the form of rents from production-sharing agreements (non-fiscal revenues). Taxes represent one-half of government revenues, but they account for only around 10 percent of Gabon's GDP. Taxes on corporate income (XAF 549 billion in the 2013 budget) have increased in recent years, reaching 17 percent of government revenues. These revenues exceeded budget forecasts in 2012 (450 billion XAF), especially for nonoil industries. This situation came about as a result of reform for better tax effectiveness. Personal income tax remains marginal (3 percent of revenues) (table 5.2).

The literature suggests that taxes can represent up to 25 percent of GDP in middle-income countries. However, in Gabon fiscal revenues represent only 10 percent of GDP. This suggests that efforts could be made to increase fiscal revenue through (i) policies to target certain subgroups for tax collection, (ii) to improve processes for tax collection, and (iii) to introduce additional taxes and levies on certain goods and services (figure 5.4).

Recently Gabon has tried to strengthen its collection of tax revenues; its track record remains below the average for middle-income countries. The government offers several tax breaks and duty exemptions that have benefited oil contracts in particular. This situation substantially limits the immediate impact on revenue. If these tax exemptions were removed, there would be additional fiscal space—without distorting the economy. Gabon's fiscal potential may also come about by increasing taxes on marginal oil contracts (see above).

Gabon has introduced innovative ways to raise funds for health. Recently, two new taxes were earmarked for the health sector to cover health expenditures for low-income groups (that is, a 1.5 percent levy on personal money transfers outside of the Central African Economic and Monetary Community (CEMAC) region and a 10 percent tax on mobile phone companies' turnover). About XAF

Table 5.2 Distribution of Government Revenues

	Absolute value (in billions XAF)	Share of government revenues (%)
Non-fiscal revenues	1,501.8	34
Oil	1,442	34
Extractive industry	59.8	0.02
Fiscal revenues	1,545	50
Corporate income tax	549	17
Personal income tax	92	3
Taxes on goods and services (VAT)	260	8.5
Custom duty	399	13
Other taxes	245	8
Loans	508	16
Total	3,554	100

Source: World Bank's calculation from Ministry of Economy Gabon data 2011.

Figure 5.4 Global Comparison of Revenue as a Share of GDP, 2009

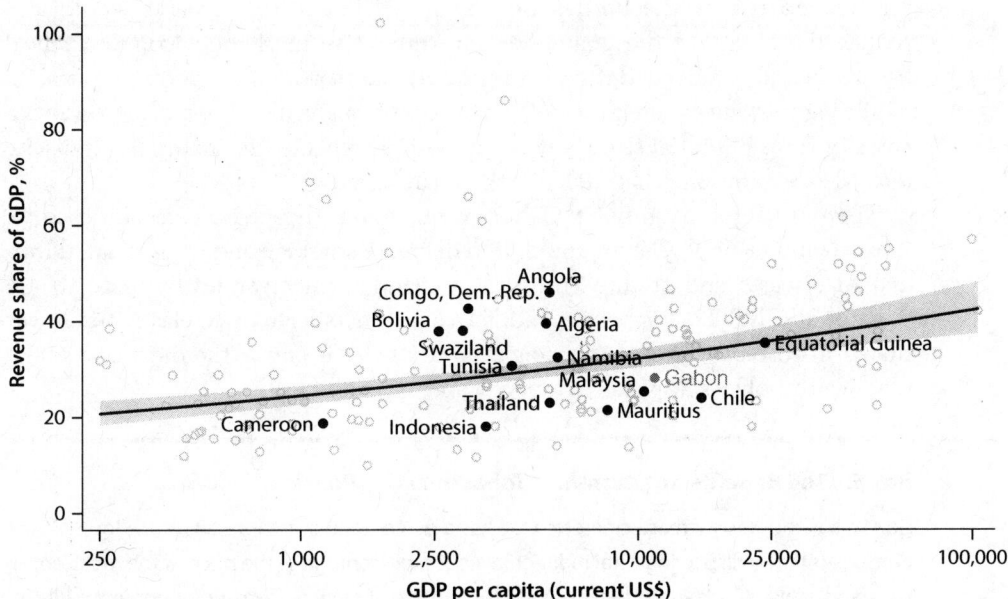

Source: World Development Indicators, WHO, updated in Apr 2014.
Note: x–axis log scale. Gray area indicates 95% confidence interval for the fitted line.

Table 5.3 National Fund for Low-Income Groups (GEF Only): Sources of Financing

billion XAF

	2008	2009
Taxes	67%	62%
Mobile phone	8.20	12.20
Remittances	0	4.00
State budget transfers	32%	37%
Subsidies for the poor	1.40	7.015
Grants for operating costs	2.50	2.760
Total resources	12.1	25.9

Source: Adapted from WHO 2009.

17 billion was allocated for CNAMGS GEF Scheme through the Redevance Obligatoire à l'Assurance Maladie (Fee Mandatory Health Insurance; ROAM) taxes in 2011. This amount is expected to stabilize (table 5.3).

The Commission for Social Affairs of the National Assembly has proposed to expand taxes to, include international bank transactions and oil contracts and to raise the value added tax (VAT) by 1.5 percent (it is now 18 percent). However, it is unlikely that new taxes will be introduced as a new source of revenues for Gabon's health sector. The political window for introducing taxes has closed due to complaints from the business community and others. Moreover, given the complexity of the current tax system, there is a greater need to simplify taxes (and yes, eliminate some) to make it easier for the tax authority to manage compliance and reduce the burden on taxpayers.[4] Excessive earmarks would also reduce the ability of the Gabonese government to implement countercyclical fiscal policy when needed, for example, during a period of economic expansion. While earmarking can help protect resources for a given sector, it also prevents a country from potential savings when growth is expected to "naturally" translate into fiscal expansion. That includes the health sector.

There is an opportunity for Gabon to reconsider the excise taxes imposed on tobacco and alcohol. Gabon could help decrease smoking and its associated burden of diseases and at the same time expand fiscal revenues by almost 0.05 percent of GDP. That is because addictive products have price elasticities lower than 1 in absolute terms. Increasing cigarette taxes is one of the most cost-effective health policies anywhere (box 5.1 and appendix C).

Box 5.1 The Benefits of Alternative Tobacco Excise Policies

Gabon has room to increase cigarette taxes as a percentage of their retail price. Figure B5.1.1 demonstrates by displaying total indirect taxes as a percentage of the price of the most-popular brand. It also displays excise taxes as a percentage of price for a group of upper middle income countries in Africa and Latin America. Angola and Gabon are the only ones with pure ad valorem taxes. Costa Rica and Brazil have a combination of specific and ad valorem rates under their excise systems. The rest of the sample has a pure specific system. Compared to this group of countries that have similar GDP per capita, in 2012 Gabon had one of the lowest indirect taxes as a percentage of price of the most popular brand. Similar to Gabon, Brazil also has a relatively low excise tax, but its VAT and other indirect taxes are high enough to ensure a high price and a high overall tax rate on cigarettes.

Figure B5.1.1 Taxes as a Percentage of the Most Popular Brand in a Set of Upper-Middle-Income Countries, 2012

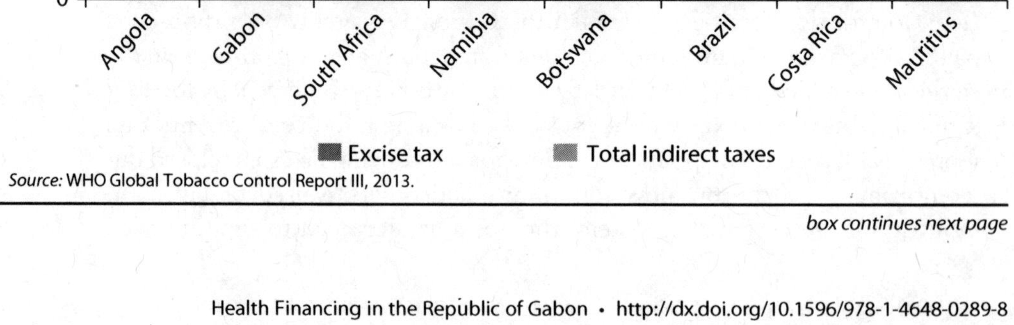

Source: WHO Global Tobacco Control Report III, 2013.

box continues next page

Box 5.1 The Benefits of Alternative Tobacco Excise Policies *(continued)*

The objective of excise taxes on tobacco products is to raise prices in relation to personal disposable income and to reduce consumption. Another way to analyze the excise tax policy on tobacco is to view the price of tobacco products relative to GDP per capita. Figure B5.1.2 presents the ratio of 100 packs of the most popular brand in 2012 to GDP per capita in the same set of upper middle income countries. Again, Gabon shows the lowest relationship of price to disposable income based on the group of comparators. This means that cigarettes are, on average, very affordable in Gabon. In short, the excise policy contributes to heavy consumption among smokers and gives youth easy access to cigarettes. A change in policy could make tobacco less affordable, which could lead to lower consumption and higher fiscal revenues.

Figure B5.1.2 Ratio of 100 Packs of the Most Popular Brand to GDP Per Capita (Percentage) in a Set of Upper-Middle-Income Countries, 2012

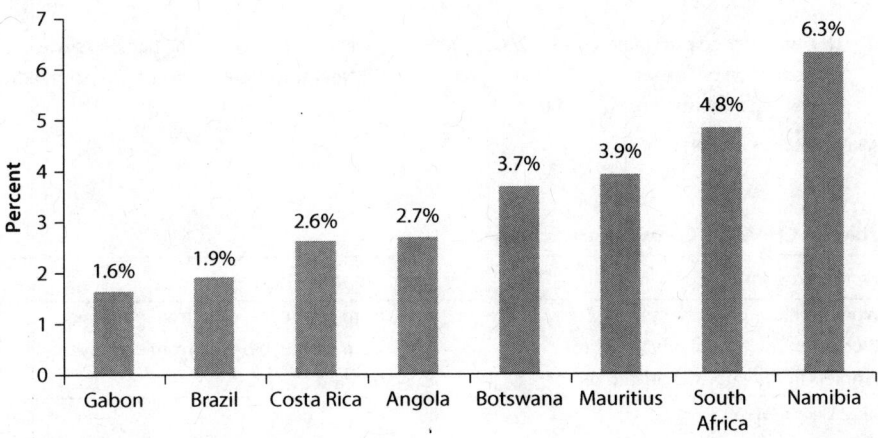

Source: WHO Global Tobacco Control Report III, 2013.

Given the preceding analysis, we recommend that the Gabonese government consider reforming and increasing tobacco taxes to reduce consumption. This step could also reduce the possibility of joining countries with a tobacco "epidemic." This step would also improve health outcomes in the short and medium terms and increase revenue from a nonproductive sector.

Source: Alejandro Ramos, Montserrat Meiro Lorenzo, Roberto Iglesias;
Note: See appendix C.

Borrowing and increasing debt for health could also be an option. The government has recently chosen to refund its debt based on a surplus from a boost in oil prices. Overall, the fiscal surplus increased from 3.4 percent in 2002 to 11.4 percent in 2008; one-half of the surpluses went to refund the external debt. As a result, external debt declined from more than 30 percent of GDP in 2007 to 15 percent in 2010. Whether the government would be willing to reopen its debt for the purpose of increasing government spending—on health—is uncertain (figure 5.5).

Figure 5.5 Use of Budget Surpluses, 2005–09

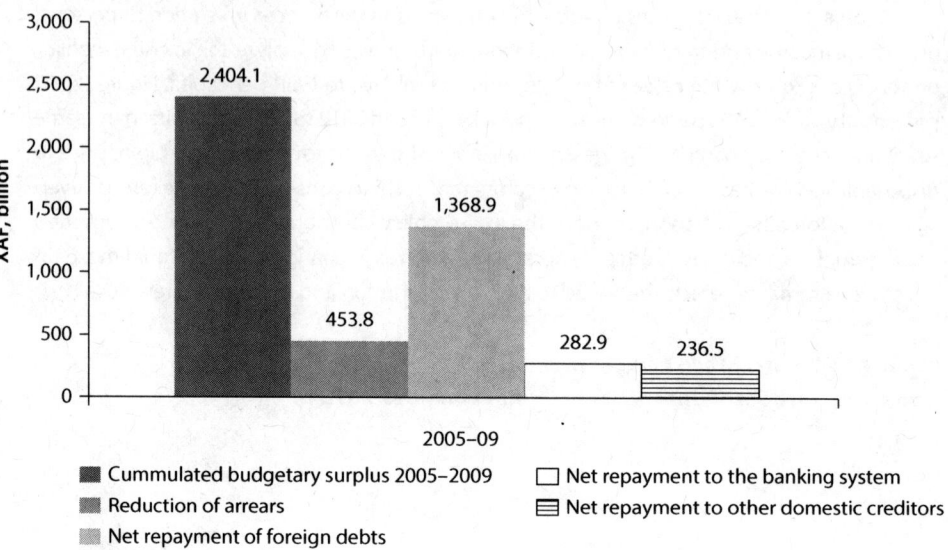

Source: Ministry of Economy, 2011.

Table 5.4 CNAMGS, Contributory Schemes

Worker category	Size of contributions
Workers in the public sector	2.5 % from employee, 4.1% from employer
Workers in the formal private sector	2.5 % from employee, 4.1% from employer
Workers in the informal private sector	To be defined

Source: Decret; WHO.

Revenues for health, especially for CNAMGS, can also come from private mandatory contributions. Gabon introduced such a measure in 2007. But, given its small population, private contributions are not expected to be a significant portion of the country's revenue (table 5.4).

Official Development Assistance for Health

Generally, official development assistance (ODA) can be another source of revenue for health. However, in Gabon, ODA represents a very low share of total health expenditure (THE); from 2000 to 2010, it was on average about 2.25 percent. That share is not expected to increase in the near future because the incomes in Gabon are static. Therefore, ODA is not a reliable source of additional revenues for health (table 5.5).

Table 5.5 Official Development Assistance as a Share of Total Health Expenditures

	2000	2001	2002	2003	2004	2005	2006	2007	2008	2009	2010
Share of ODA in THE (%)	2.6	2.3	1.8	1.6	1.9	2.5	3.0	2.7	2.3	1.7	2.4

Source: WHO/MOHPH.
Note: ODA = official development assistance; THE = total health expenditure.

Increasing Efficiency of Government Health Spending

In general, fiscal space can be realized by gains in efficiency. In most settings improvements in allocative and technical efficiency have the potential to free up substantial resources for health.[5] Based on empirical evidence, Mathonnat demonstrates that in a sample of 84 low and lower middle-income countries, gains in efficiency (*output-oriented*[6]) have the potential to generate greater fiscal space for health than any other policy or fiscal alternative.

Based on our analysis, realizing gains in efficiency from both public and private spending must be a priority for Gabon before or in parallel with injecting additional resources into the sector. Gabon's health's performance—infant mortality is one critical example—is low based on income status and total health spending. A shift in government spending for health is also critical. Additional funding needs to go to primary and preventive care so that the neediest members of the population will benefit. Furthermore, a shift from supply-side financing to the demand-side is necessary for the government to increasingly be able to subsidize the costs of the poorest (GEF). Earmarked taxes are not expected to be enough to cover the overall bill. Reprioritization *within* the health budget is also expected to generate resources for priority interventions.

Summary

In conclusion, the greatest opportunities to expand the fiscal space for health in Gabon are economic growth and the establishment of new priorities for health in the government budget. Economic growth could yield an additional 8–15 percent; establishing new priorities for health may bring in about 4 percent of additional resources. ODA and new taxes are not likely to expand the fiscal space for health in the near future. Furthermore, because enrollment of the nonpoor is at an early phase, there is a degree of uncertainty regarding CNAMGS premium-based revenues. Finally, improving the system's efficiency can release large portions of fiscal space. Though hard to quantify, the focus should be on reforming expenditure management, implementing effective cost-control strategies and upgrading the quality of service (table 5.6).

Table 5.6 Summary of Options for Generating Fiscal Space for Health

Sources of fiscal space for health	Potential for generating additional fiscal space for health	Conditions
Growth in income	Moderate	If International Monetary Fund projections are realized and elasticity of government health spending to GDP increases
Reprioritization of health within the budget	Moderate	If the budget's share for health is increased to at least 8 percent of the total government expenditure
Additional earmarks resources for health	Limited	Limited window due to reduced prospects for tax collection
Efficiency	Large	Due to the low level of output for the level of high input, Gabon can generate substantial resources by making public and private spending more efficient.

Source: World Bank.
Note: GDP = gross domestic product.

Notes

1. In preparing this chapter, the author reviewed the most recent macroeconomic data (World Development Indicators, World Bank; International Monetary Fund). But this chapter does not explore the political feasibility of the proposed options.

2. World Bank's estimation based on budget execution rates and actual government spending.

3. WHO. WHO Report on the Global Tobacco Epidemic, 2013. Country Profile: Gabon. The reports shows that packs of cigarettes currently have a total tax of about 35 percent (2012); 15.3 percent is VAT and 19.6 percent is excise taxes. But there may be potential for additional revenue, which could be estimated.

4. World Bank. 2013. Report on the tax burden.

5. Mathonnat 2010 and for literature on economic efficiency in health: Alexander, Busch, and Stringer (2003), Bokhari, Gai, and Gottret (2007), Estache, Gonzalez, and Trujillo (2007), Filmer and Prichett (1999), Gupta and Verhoeven (2001), Herrera (2005).

6. Outputs orientation—by contrast with inputs orientation—signals that more health outputs are expected for a given level of inputs.

CHAPTER 6

Key Reform Issues and Policy Options

Introduction

This chapter highlights key reform issues and policy options concerning health financing in Gabon. These reforms focus on public sector financing and Caisse Nationale d'Assurance Maladie et de Garantie Sociale (National Health Insurance and Social Security; CNAMGS). The first section briefly discusses a few structural issues that directly affect the funding, organization and provision of health care services. The second section reviews some issues where allocative and technical efficiencies could be gained. The third section provides some reform options for CNAMGS. The fourth section provides some global lessons that may benefit Gabon, and future agenda for additional assessments.

Key Reform Issues

Having undertaken various health finance reforms over the years—ranging from user fees to free health care under a national health service—Gabon has embarked on demand-side financing when it launched the National Health Insurance Program (NHIP) in 2007. With the introduction of the NHIP, additional funds have gone to the health sector from taxes and private contributions. Although Gabon's per capita health spending is close to the spending patterns of countries with similar incomes, its health outcomes remain poor.

Gabon aims to improve the health outcomes of its people. The country has also committed to achieving universal health coverage. Because of these two goals, certain segments of society are clamoring for additional resources for the sector. As a result, the country is grappling with three fundamental questions: how resources are being spent, whether there is room for a more efficient allocation of current resources, and whether there is an immediate need to mobilize additional resources to meet its goals.

Structural Issues in Governance, Resource Management and Incentives

This section reviews issues of governance, regulations, planning, and budgeting. It also highlights incentive structures that are constraining the health sector's efficiency.

Weak sector governance: Fragmentation and overlap between Ministry of Health and Public Hygiene (MOHPH) and the NHIP (under the Ministry of Economy) have weakened governance of the health sector. The health system also lacks a clear and shared vision. MOHPH's leadership and its capacity for policy making are weak; the split and overlap with CNAMGS (and until recently Caisse Nationale de Securité Sociale [CNSS]) has raised additional challenges, worsened by pressure from the Ministry of Economy. Furthermore, strong mechanisms for sector coordination are also lacking. The views of the Ministry of Economy and MOHPH conflict with one another. The latter complains about the lack of funding; meanwhile, the Ministry of Economy remains convinced that "health is too expensive." As a result, its funds go for the wrong services. In fact, both views are correct. The country gets little return on its investment in health care and facility operations suffer from chronic underfunding. To address this issue, it is critical to establish a clear mechanism for sector coordination and a comprehensive review and revision of each sector's priorities and their sectoral allocation mechanisms.

Policy, planning and implementation: A structured planning and budgeting system is in place. However, it suffers from substantial limitations. First, plans and budgets are not implemented as planned. Further, many reform initiatives are never carried out. This is due to MOHPH's weak capacity for policy making, its poor implementation capacity and the lack of a long-term vision for Gabon's health sector. Second, the inability to predict budget allocations and disbursements leads to a lack of credibility for the budget and planning process in general. Third, foggy and conflicting patterns of centralization/decentralization give facility managers too much freedom in some areas—with no clear accountability or appropriate supervision. At the same time, the present state of affairs restricts their ability to make critical decisions when it comes to allocating resources. The government is in the process of implementing a system for output-based budgeting, but that innovation alone is unlikely to solve or address these issues.

Weak regulation and norms: The Gabon health sector also suffers from an inadequate regulatory framework. While a number of regulations and norms exist, many have not been implemented, much less published. Consequently, staff at the facility level are unaware of them. Equally important, many aspects of facility operations take place in a regulatory void. Each facility decides how to manage specific processes—without general policies, norms, or guidance in place. Facilities do so despite the lack of qualified staff to make these decisions. As a result, there is an absence of uniformity at the facility level.

Ineffective staff incentives: Basic staff remuneration in the public sector is low.[1] However, personnel in public health facilities are paid several additional amounts based on location, working hours, function or responsibility. In addition, a substantial incentive bonus is paid monthly. To add to the muddle, recent regulations and a presidential speech have sent conflicting messages to facility managers and staff as well as accountants and auditors that work for different oversight agencies.[2] In the absence of regulations by MOHPH, facilities have applied their own interpretations of the legislation.

Performance-based incentives. In any case, the current system of additional staff payments and bonuses provides no incentives to improve performance or the quality of care. They are not linked to clear measures of performance. As a result, there are wide differences in staff behavior across facilities. In some, strong personal leadership ensures staff are present and working. In others most of the staff are absent or do not appear to be productive.

Provider incentives: Provider incentives are not aligned with policies or priorities for two reasons. First, a conflicting pattern of centralization/decentralization does not provide a clear framework for facility managers to operate within. For instance, several hospitals have partially outsourced their operations to a private company to improve facility management. Instead, hospital management has to comply with inefficient and rigid procurement rules (for example for drugs) that greatly reduce its ability to make genuine improvements.

For the health delivery system to be more effective there is need to revisit the situation in the country on the stewardship role, the regulatory frameworks, accountability mechanisms, and incentive structures in place. Health system strengthening has to go hand in hand with addressing the overall governance issues in the country.

How Can Gabon's Health Spending Achieve Value for the Money?

First, Gabon can examine those areas that cause inefficiencies in allocations and spending. This step could save precious resources. According to the World Health Organization (WHO), as much as 20–40 percent of health resources are wasted because of inefficiencies. Second, it would help if Gabon were to identify its cost drivers and consider ways to control them. Third, Gabon needs to consider ways to mobilize resources that are sustainable.

Technical Efficiency
Inefficient mix of health interventions (for example prevention versus treatment). Immunization coverage could be improved. The same is true of the use of bednets. Appropriate interventions exist to control malaria, but they are not widespread. Public health is still underresourced. Funds, staffing, and community based public health programs are inadequate. Facility-based programs that emphasize treatment receive more attention than much needed community-based prevention programs. A shift in priorities in favor of prevention, early detection and screening could help reduce human immunodeficiency virus (HIV), tuberculosis (TB), malaria, and preventable childhood diseases. Public health programs, such as sanitation, needs to be urgently addressed.

Inappropriate or costly staff-mix. Staff are concentrated in hospitals and urban areas. To address the current disease burden, community-based health care and primary health care should be strengthened along a robust referral network to go with them. Gabon has health workers, such as nurses and midwives, who with the appropriate training, could be deployed to community-based settings, and primary care facilities. Community-based workers are also needed for local programs. To build a health delivery system, referral networks will have to address maternal and child emergency care services more than they do now. Primary health workers and primary health care programs should be less expensive than hospital-based health services, and thereby a strengthened primary health care would save on unnecessary costs.

Unmotivated health workers. A recent staff audit showed that as much as 10 percent of staff are absent. Many health facilities in Gabon have a surplus of staff; others are understaffed. Although a bonus system exists, it is not clear what impact it has on staff. Gabon should review this program for that reason. There may be an opportunity to create an incentive mechanism that is performance based.

Inappropriate hospital size. The country has made considerable investments in hospital; in fact, there is an excess of hospital beds. Many hospitals have occupancy rates as low as 40 percent. If some of these hospitals merged or some hospital beds convert to primary health care centers for maternal and child care and for emergency care, that could reduce some inefficiencies. Further, many regional hospitals do not have appropriate specialists. Merging hospitals or creating a more effective rotation program among specialists could also help reduce cost inefficiencies. It might also encourage patients to go to facilities that are nearby rather than bypassing lower level facilities in favor of higher level hospitals.

Inappropriate and ineffective use of medicines. Pharmaceutical spending has grown since the inception of the NHIP. That suggests the increase is due to the introduction of the NHIP. Although CNAMGS promotes generics and branded generics, there is a need to identify what is causing this increase in pharmaceutical spending. Fee-for-service payments are known to result in supply-induced demand. It could have also triggered providers to prescribe more expensive or more inappropriate drugs. Also, staffing norms on pharmacists, may force patients to purchase drugs from private pharmacies and encounter balance billing.

Patients bypassing primary health care clinics in favor of hospitals. Patients are bypassing primary care clinics in favor of hospitals in search of quality care. Primary care clinics are underresourced in funding, staffing, and equipment. A strengthened primary care system would lead to an overall increase in patient flow and lower costs for the health system and patients. While NHIP and its reimbursements to providers could have had a potential to improve primary care level services, the poor quality of care offered at these facilities have deterred patients from using these facilities. Thereby, these facilities benefit little from demand side financing. One solution is to increase investments directly into primary care facilities through budget. With improved quality of care, maintaining the investments would follow from the reimbursements received from NHIP.

Limited information for decision making. Gabon relies on household-based surveys to monitor progress in the health sector. Institutional information systems exist, but they have limited data. The MOHPH has established a department of health management information system (Cellule d'Observation de la Santé Publique [COSP]). Efforts are underway to create population-based data and geographical information systems (GIS). An ehealth strategy is necessary to enhance surveillance systems as well as facility based information systems. Although CNAMGS has ehealth to register beneficiaries, an electronic claims (eclaims) system would improve with the efficiency of insurance claims management and timely reimbursement.

Allocative Efficiency

Limited investments in cost-effective interventions such as family planning programs. Contraceptive use is low although the need for it is significant. Abortion rates are also significant and one of the causes of maternal deaths. While this study could not undertake a situation analysis for family planning, the country would gain from establishing a priority for contraceptives in its basic benefits package (subsidized by MOHPH or covered by the CNAMGS). These commodities and services are readily accessible and affordable. The use of contraceptives has multiple benefits, including the spacing of births and maternal health. This investment would gain value for money.

Limited investments in primary health care in favor of hospitals. Primary health care, including community based programs, is not widespread. Primary health care is underresourced with limited funds, limited staffing, and limited access. Effective primary health care can reduce costs and provide appropriate and timely treatment. It is key to improving health outcomes. Primary health care could be strengthened to address communicable diseases, maternal and child health, and the prevention and early detection of noncommunicable and diseases associated with lifestyle. Funding for primary and preventive care needs to be a higher priority. If that occurred, it would benefit the lower levels of care and presumably the neediest. This step could also lead to greater efficiency of allocations. This investment would gain value for money.

Limited recurrent health budgets for maintenance, outreach programs, etc. The budget is based on inputs, not outputs or needs. Insufficient funds are available for operations, maintenance and programs. As more population are enrolled into NHIP, and as more services are used, including for primary health care, the reimbursements from NHIP would provide the additional resources needed for operations and maintenance.

Inequity in per capita budgeting for regions or districts. Further, allocations are based on inputs, such as hospitals, staff, and others rather than population or gaps in services. Budget allocations based on need and equity is in order.

Execution of health budgets is low. In recent years, as little as 70 percent of the health budget was actually carried out. Contributing factors include: an insufficient budget formulation and preparation process, lack of budget execution and procurement tools. There is clearly an opportunity to explore options to improve budget execution in health in a shorter time frame by improving budget planning and monitoring processes with appropriate tools.

Issues and Reform Options under CNAMGS

There is a need to ensure some or all of the following for a more efficient, affordable and financially sustainable health program that delivers on its commitment to universal health coverage. This section highlights some issues and reform options for consideration by the government in the medium-term (see table 6.1 for summary; see Appendix D for short- and medium-term reform considerations.):

Table 6.1 Some Summary Reform Options for CNAMGS

Issues	Options
Increase enrollment	Ensure those enrolled in GEF are those who are the poor (means/proxy means tested). Ensure premium subsidies can be maintained for GEF beneficiaries.
	Identify informal sector workers, incentives for them to register and/or government subsidies for their premiums.
	Ensure private sector workers regard enrollment in the public scheme as beneficial. They have other options that may provide better health services.
Cost controls/efficiency gains	Supplier-induced demand is a result of fee for service payment. Monitor how it is affecting the use of services and prescription practices.
	Consider capitation for primary health care.
	Release reimbursements on a timely manner.
	Conduct validation/technical audits of claims.
	Pool schemes to reduce unnecessary administrative costs associated with running separate schemes.
	Promote generics and ensure prices approximate international drug reference pricing.
	Increase accreditation of private providers.
	Improve the quality of care (and thereby actual accreditation) of public providers.
	Re-assess the benefits package and its costs.
	Review the policy on tariffs.
	Improve ICT for claims management.
Financial sustainability	Ensure the timely release of funds from treasury to CNAMGS. This matter is of special concern for the sustainability of the two funds—GEF Fund and the civil servant's Fund—both of which rely on public sector contributions.
	Ensure sources of financing are sustainable in light of growth projections.
	Premiums charged are based on actuarial estimates.
	Ensure a policy is in place for reserves.
Financial protection	Re-consider copayment policies for GEF beneficiaries.
	Regularize NHA.
	Improve monitoring systems.

Source: World Bank.
Note: Refer to appendix D. CNAMGS = Caisse Nationale d´Assurance Maladie et de Garantie Sociale; GEF = Gabonais Economiquement Faibles; ICT = information and communication technology; NHA = National Health Accounts.

Eligibility of low-income groups: To be eligible for a health insurance subsidy, an adult must earn less than XAF 80,000 a month ($160), equal to the monthly minimum wage in Gabon. A national census was used to elaborate on the list of beneficiaries. Because means tests were difficult to administer, the current list reportedly contains errors and is likely to include wealthier quintiles. There is also discussion around changing eligibility criteria, including the possibility of an entire household, rather than individual incomes. Proposals to target government subsidies to the truly indigent are not only commendable but they also free up resources and reinforce equity and financial protections.

Improving enrollment compliance and the collection of premiums: Enrollment remains incomplete. If it can be increased, it will automatically generate additional resources and reduce the administrative costs associated with CNAMGS's operations. Although the transfer of CNSS to CNAMGS posed a major obstacle (politically, financially and technically) to the successful enrollment of the private sector, apparently both parties are ready to move forward. It is anticipated that additional resources will be forthcoming by 2015. Still, the scope of contributions from the private sector remains uncertain. It is essential that the government quantify potential gaps in CNAMGS's budget.

Source of financing for the coverage of informal sector workers under CNAMGS: While CNAMGS appears to be moving quickly to register the poor, civil servants and workers in the private sector, there is little momentum to cover informal sector workers; no specific scheme is in place for them, nor is one planned. Registration of informal sector workers is voluntary and there is little incentive for them to enroll. Lessons from other countries suggest that coverage of informal sector workers may be a challenge. More than 70 percent of Gabon's population comes from the informal sector. Often countries like Ghana and the Philippines have had registrations stalled because workers in the informal sector are hard to reach. Thailand on the other hand decided to subsidize the premiums of all informal sector workers under general taxes. There are pros and cons, subsidizing informal sector could motivate the formal sector to increase informality (as seen in the Philippines), however, (partial or full) subsidies may help increase enrollment.

Gabon will have to figure out how to offer an incentive for these workers to register. Critical questions that might help CNAMGS develop a policy are as follows: Is there a demand? Who will pay the premiums? Will there be government subsidies, how much? And what will be the source of financing? CNAMGS plans to develop a strategy in 2015 and 2016 for covering informal sector workers.

The benefit package: The benefit package under CNAMGS is comprehensive (outpatient, inpatient, and drugs) but curative in nature. It excludes those goods and services that are communicable, covered by the MOHPH or through external grant financing. It is imperative to ensure public health objectives are equally met and its coverage accelerated. Further, the benefit package under CNAMGS includes nonhealth coverage, such as a childbirth bonus and school spending for children up to 18 years of age. The CNAMGS premiums are not based on an actuarial estimate, and so it not clear whether sufficient revenue is collected to cover the costs of care. However, an actuarial and financial sustainability analysis is planned for 2014 and 2015.

Provider payment mechanism and the incentives for supplier-induced demand: CNAMGS uses a fee-for-service payment mechanism for services and for drugs at all types of facilities (health clinics to hospitals). This mechanism is known to result in supplier- induced demand. Service use has gone up; however, specifics are yet to be determined. This study was unable to collect information on how the pattern of services has changed. However, claims expenditures have increased significantly as a share of total CNAMGS spending and in per capita terms (see figure 4.4). Incentives arising from payment mechanisms are often distorted; for example, the high level of C-sections is clearly linked to the fact that providers receive a higher amount for them than normal deliveries. Other provider payment mechanism options can be considered such as capitation at primary health care and case-mix payment at hospitals (table 6.2).

Is gatekeeping an option?: The existing payment system for the 80 contracted hospitals and health centers is based on fixed tariffs for every service delivered.[3] In the absence of a clear cost-monitoring and regulatory mechanism, it is likely that this payment system will reinforce the fiscal fragility of the CNAMGS. Introducing a hybrid payment system, through case-mix activity-based payment and fixed support budgets, could be a solid strategy for controlling costs. Encouraging clients to use primary care as an entry point (through gate keepers for example) is another potential means to free up resources. However, in both case, the primary attention will need to be given to upgrading quality of care.

Copayments and their effect on offering financial protection against the cost of illness: The country still does not offer financial protection. Much more is expected of an upper-middle-income country (UMIC) that aims to achieve universal health coverage. CNAMGS claims to have achieved universal health insurance coverage among the poor. However, CNAMGS's policy on copayments for medical services and drugs needs further assessment. Although the policy was introduced to reduce moral hazard, it could also result in significant household spending on health, especially by the poor and near poor. It is noteworthy that many of its beneficiaries are visiting hospitals for consultations instead of clinics. Travelling to urban centers to access hospitals adds to travel costs. Charges for similar consultation services at hospitals are higher than at clinics. Balance billing also exists in private health facilities. Although most of the poor do not use private health facilities, when they do, their health care costs could be even higher. Given the lack of household income-expenditure surveys, it is not clear what households spend on health. A benefit incidence analysis would provide an even better understanding of who benefits from government subsidies, but that analysis is not possible given limited information. However, a poverty survey at the household level is expected to be conducted in 2015 and could help with a benefit incidence analysis.

Table 6.2 Provider Payment Mechanisms: Payment Method, Effects and Country Examples

	Payment method	Effects	Country examples
Primary health care	Line-item budget: fixed amount for inputs	Strong cost control; risk for under-provision	UK in the 1980s, former Soviet Union republics, currently: Egypt, Arab Rep., the Philippines, Vietnam, Bangladesh, Mozambique....
	Fee-for-service: payment based on the number of services delivered (with agreed fee schedule or retrospective cost-based payment)	Incentive for overprovision and costly services	France, Canada, China, Japan, Korea, Rep., United States (under indemnity plans), Austria, Germany, most African countries
	Capitation: pre-defined rate for each resident enrolled	Output based; can attract additional enrollees; cost-control; risk for under-provision; risk for patient selection	United Kingdom, Spain (for GPs)
Hospital and acute care	Global budget: determined by historical expenditures	Cost control; risk for underprovision; no incentive for productivity; facility deficits	Formerly France (for public hospitals), Ireland (case-mix adjustment to global budgets)
	Case-mix payment: reimbursed per diagnosis-related groups[a]	Incentive for volume; can improve efficiency (length of stay); shift to ambulatory strategies, risk for selection of low cost patients, question for appropriateness of care)	United States (first DRG system), Australia, France (since 2007), Germany, Switzerland, Brazil, Thailand, Hungary, Slovenia. Pilots in Indonesia, Vietnam, Korea, Rep., and China.
	Per-diem payment: daily payment	Increase length of stay and number of admissions	Formerly Germany, Brazil (in the 1970s), Estonia (coupled with budget cap)

Source: World Bank.
Note: Adapted from Langenbrunner, Cashin and O'Dougherty 2009 and Park et al. 2007.
a. DRGs are a patient classification system developed to classify users into groups economically and medically similar, expected to have similar use of healthcare service and related costs.

Claims processing: CNAMGS has introduced electronic health systems (ehealth) to register beneficiaries. However, it has not yet introduced a comprehensive system that includes an electronic claims (eclaims) management system. Claims are processed manually. Providers indicate that reimbursements are often delayed. These delays could be a result of multiple factors: low releases from the treasury to CNAMGS, insufficient reserves, or manual claims processing. Because many providers rely heavily on off-budget for their operating costs, a delay in reimbursement can be very disruptive to a facility. Further assessment is required. That includes the development of an audit/fraud management cell to ensure the validation of claims.

Cross subsidization: CNAMGS has three different schemes: (i) for the poor; (ii) for civil servants and the formal sector, (iii) for the informal sector. With such institutional arrangements, it is unlikely that risk will be shared and effective cross-subsidization between the rich and poor and the healthy and the sick will occur. To ensure both progressivity and efficiency, it is highly recommended to (i) pool the risks for the general population and the poor, or (ii) set up formulas for cross-subsidization transfers between the different pools.

Financial sustainability of health insurance: The health insurance scheme was established to ensure universal coverage. Coverage has been greatly and successfully expanded. Nevertheless, the schemes are fragmented and there are no clear plans for a pooling mechanism to allow cross-subsidization. Furthermore, there is a lack of consistent cost estimates and no systematic actuarial study to ensure that each scheme is sustainable. As CNAMGS moves forward to establish new insurance schemes for population groups that are still not covered and it seeks to identify additional sources of funding for them, CNAMGS should first consider a comprehensive actuarial study of the current and proposed schemes.

Upgrading the quality of service and re-orienting budget subsidies: Inadequate quality of service creates unnecessary costs for the system (bypassing, follow-up visits, false prescribing patterns, over-use of high-cost services) and ultimately for patient's health outcomes. Gabon has made significant investment in responding to concerns of low quality care. It is necessary to elaborate on those efforts by focusing on primary and preventive care. To improve service coverage may require redistributing some of government health spending to lower levels of care (that is primary and preventive) so that those who are worse off may benefit more from government subsidies than is true today. Performance-based payments may also be an option for boosting the quality of service. Accreditation may be another; few nonpublic facilities in Gabon are accredited.

Lessons to Be Learnt from Other Countries Around the Globe

This section provides some case studies of countries that can benefit Gabon. We have selected case studies that used innovative mechanisms to strengthen primary health care as well as improve accountability, efficiency, and equity.

The Case of Brazil—Performance Contract

Making managers and staff accountable for the performance of their facility usually occurs when combining two basic tools: contracting and performance-based financing. For example, Brazil's public health system (Sistema Único de Saúde SUS (Unified National Health System), which is responsible for two-thirds of the country's ambulatory care and hospital admissions) suffered from low performance and poor accountability for a long time. However, since the mid-90s, SUS has gradually moved away from paying public providers on the basis of line-item budgeting and private providers on fee-for-service. The first step was to establish a contract between the Ministry of Health and regional (state) and local (municipalities) to provide primary health care (PHC). The contract was based on a mixed payment system which included a flat per capita payment and variable payments linked to specific target indicators. The PHC included coverage by the newly launched Family Health Program (FHP). This approach represented a radical change from in the way the PHC was organized. Its innovative financing mechanisms were highly successful; they became an international model. FHP coverage rapidly increased to reach 50 percent of the population (90 million people); in a little more than 10 years, infant mortality dropped by 50 percent. More recently, SUS has gradually applied the same concept to public and private hospitals. Under one particularly successful model, namely the social organizations in the state of São Paulo, the government has engaged private nonprofit organizations to run and manage public hospitals under a performance contract. Payments under this contract combine a global budget mechanism with a variable that is linked to achieving specific targets.[4]

The Case of Malaysia—Public-Private Partnership

Under Malaysia's 2006–10 Ninth Development Plan, poverty eradication programs reduced poverty from 5.7 percent in 2005 to 3.8 percent in 2009. In addition, education and health conditions were significantly improved (see figure 6.1). Recognizing that "health is an important asset in the development of human capital" and that "a healthy society contributes to a dynamic and productive nation," the government has strengthened one of the best health systems in Southeast Asia by promoting public-private partnerships as a way to improve access to health services, coverage, and quality of care. Using regional WHO comparators, Malaysia fares well in terms of providing universal health care to all its citizens. Its total health expenditure is close to 5 percent of gross domestic product (GDP). Out-of-pocket payments are roughly one-third of total health expenditures. Comprehensive social safety nets are in place for vulnerable people and a tax-based financing system serves as a national risk pool for the population.[5]

Based on the experience of these countries, it is clear that the structure of a health system reflects what kind of society a country wants to have. Broad social goals will ultimately guide policy and institutional decisions concerning the most appropriate and contextually relevant organizational forms, health care financing arrangements, and service delivery mechanisms that could be adopted to attain the intermediate goals of a health system (improved access, quality, efficiency,

Figure 6.1 Malaysia, GNI Per Capita, School Enrollment, and Under-5 Mortality Rate

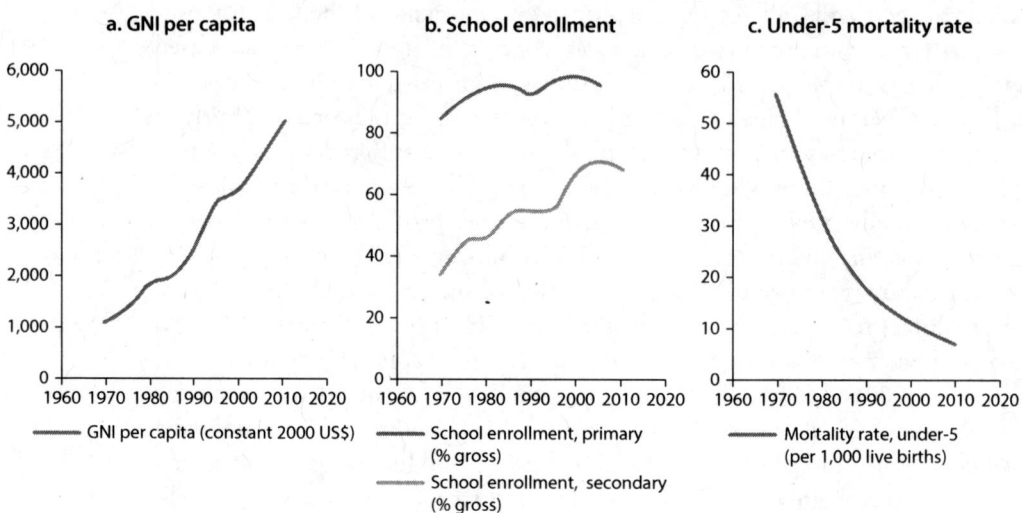

Source: World Bank. 2013a. Africa Health Forum: finance and capacity for results. Chapter on "How to translate mineral wealth into health and social development."

and fairness). These contribute to achieving the ultimate goals of a health system (improved health status, financial protection, and patient satisfaction with the care they received).

The Case of Results Based Financing—RBF Strengthens Key Health System Functions

Accountability: Results-based financing (RBF) programs make health systems more accountable by shifting the focus from inputs to results. Linking payments to performance strengthens the governance of the system. It also allows ongoing monitoring of the results that government and partner resources are 'buying.' There is strong evidence that linking financing to results produces better outcomes than similar financing without these links. Figure 6.2 shows the impact on health facilities in Zambia.

Efficiency: RBF can be used to improve efficiency in the health system. For example, by setting the payments high for services (such as deliveries) performed at health centers, RBF increases efficiency by allowing hospital resources to be used for complicated care. This has been the experience in Zimbabwe (figure 6.3). In Rwanda, RBF reduced by 20 percent the gap between provider knowledge and the practice of appropriate clinical procedures (Gertler and Vermeersch 2012).

Equity: There are multiple channels by which RBF programs can improve equity. Many programs offer a bonus to facilities in remote areas. In Burundi, program investment has allowed remote provinces to catch up with those that are better off in terms of improving quality of care. As shown in figure 6.4, the variation in quality of care across provinces narrows over time.

Figure 6.2 Zambia, Increase in Coverage of Institutional Deliveries in Districts with Performance-Based Financing and Districts with Input-Based Financing

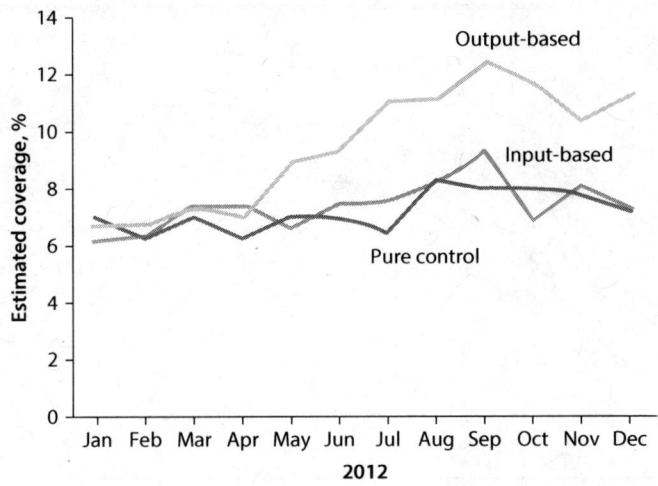

Source: World Bank. 2013a. Africa Health Forum: finance and capacity for results. Chapter on "Results-Based Financing for Health."

Figure 6.3 Zimbabwe, Increase in Number of Deliveries at Primary Care Level

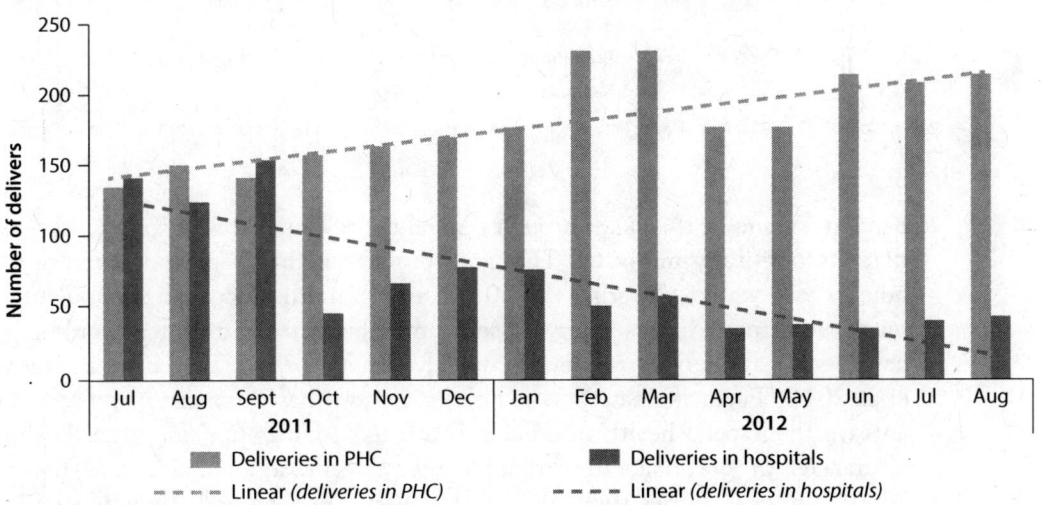

Source: World Bank. 2013a. Africa Health Forum: finance and capacity for results. Chapter on "Results-Based Financing for Health."

The Case of Thailand—Inclusion of the Nonpoor Informal Sector into the NHIP

Countries that make transfers from general revenues have seen coverage rates improve significantly and relatively quickly. For example, after introducing its universal coverage scheme (UCS),[6] Thailand saw coverage climb to nearly 100

Health Financing in the Republic of Gabon • http://dx.doi.org/10.1596/978-1-4648-0289-8

Figure 6.4 Burundi, Improved Quality Scores over Time and Reduced Variation/Greater Equity

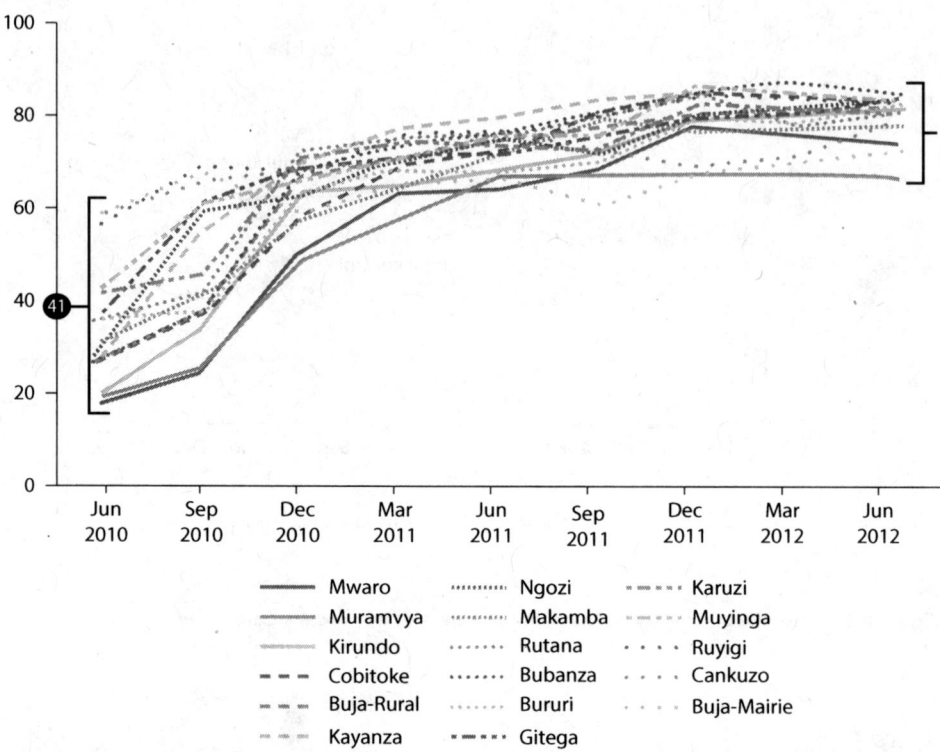

—— Mwaro	·········· Ngozi	—· —· Karuzi
—— Muramvya	·········· Makamba	—· —· Muyinga
—— Kirundo	······· Rutana	· · · · Ruyigi
— — — Cobitoke	······· Bubanza	· · · · Cankuzo
— — — Buja-Rural	······· Bururi	· · · · Buja-Mairie
—· —· Kayanza	·—·— Gitega	

Source: World Bank. 2013a. Africa Health Forum: finance and capacity for results. Chapter on "Results-Based Financing for Health."

percent. Financing the UCS through general tax revenues was pragmatic—given that the politically motivated Thai government sought to expand coverage as quickly as possible. Covering the 30 percent formerly noncovered population mostly informal workers using a distinct membership contribution would not have been feasible or carried out as quickly (Li et al. 2011; Tangcharoensathien et al. 2011). Financing based on income or an asset-based tax can be more progressive than social health insurance. The usual contribution for social health insurance is proportionate to current income subject to a cap or a flat rate (Kwon 2009).[7] Other countries, such as China, Hungary, Moldova, and others, have over time reverted to a greater reliance on general revenues to cover their informal sectors (Wagstaff et al. 2009; Kutzin, Cashin, and Jakab 2010).[8]

The Case of the Philippines—Tobacco Tax to Fund NHIP

As of 1 January 2013, Republic Act No. 10351, which restructured the excise tax on alcohol and tobacco products, has been in force in the Philippines. The tax on cigarettes is now 12 Philippine pesos (P12), approximately $ 0.3 per pack for those with a net retail price (excluding the excise tax and the 12 percent value added tax) of P11.50 and below. For those with a higher retail price, the tax is P25. The rates will go up to P17 and P27, respectively, in 2014, P21 and P28 in 2015, and P25 and P29 in 2016. There will be a single rate of P30 per pack starting in 2017. This rate will rise by 4 percent every year thereafter.

Under the old law there were four categories of cigarettes based on their retail prices and tax rates. Now there are just two. Beginning in 2017, the new law provides for a uniform tax treatment. The old levies ranged from P2 per pack for low-priced cigarettes to P28 for those classified as premium.

The law also allocates 15 percent of incremental revenue collected from the excise tax to programs that would benefit tobacco farmers switching to alternative livelihoods. Of the remaining 85 percent, 80 percent will be allocated to universal health care under the national health insurance program, the attainment of the Millennium Development Goal (MDG) and health awareness programs. The remaining 20 percent will be allocated to political and district subdivisions for medical assistance and health enhancement facilities nationwide. The Department of Health[9] will determine these requirements on an annual basis.

Recommendations for Future Studies

Public expenditure assessments could provide a better understanding of spending patterns over time and the performance that goes with them. It is not clear where public sector resources in Gabon are going and whether the government is optimizing the returns on its investments in health programs and initiatives. The government could explore the possibility of instituting a "Return on investment (ROI) system" designed to improve program performance and assist in making mid-course corrections. This would complement the findings of the National Health Accounts. The recent Public Expenditure review also provides an insight to understanding some of the overall challenges to public expenditure management, and the government's plans to move to output based budgeting.

Actuarial analysis is critical to assess the feasibility of a health insurance program. Gabon has decided to offer a comprehensive health insurance program to all. Gabon had separate health insurance programs covering various groups, including the vulnerable, civil servants and formal sector workers. These groups are now consolidated under CNAMGS. So far, no actuarial analysis has taken place. CNSS and CNAMGS rely on in-house projections alone. These projections were conducted in 2007 when the CNAMGS program began. A formal actuarial analysis (by a qualified actuary) is critically needed. The analysis should examine the following: coverage, benefits package, purchasing, service use, cost drivers, and financial sustainability.

Public Expenditure Tracking Survey and health service delivery assessment. In countries with weak institutions, budget allocations alone can be a poor indicator of the quality and quantity of public services. Although shifting budgetary resources to priority sectors like education and health is a good first step, it is crucial to ascertain where and how the allocations get spent. Public Expenditure

Health Financing in the Republic of Gabon • http://dx.doi.org/10.1596/978-1-4648-0289-8

Tracking Surveys (PETS) are quantitative exercises that trace the flow of resources from their origin to their destination; they also determine the location and scale of anomaly. PETS is a diagnostic tool that tracks the flow of resources from the central government through line ministries (for example, MOHPH) and intermediary administrative levels (provinces, districts) to the service delivery unit (for example, hospital or clinic). It can capture elements of: budget allocations such as timeliness of funding, local discretion in the use of resources, degree of leakage; comparison of resources at each level (if possible, vis-à-vis performance); reasons for variances; assessment of "fiduciary risk"—risk that resources are not accounted for or are not used for their intended purposes. PETS highlight not only the use and abuse of public money, but it can also offer insight to the concepts of capture, cost efficiency, decentralization, and accountability. In the absence of a strong institutional infrastructure to manage the flow of information, tracking surveys offer a realistic portrayal of the status of demand and supply of services. This diagnostic tool can also justify a need for creating cost effective mechanisms for public accountability by disseminating information on the use and allocation of resources.

Benefit incidence analysis for health. Governments want health subsidies (that is government health spending [GHS]) to disproportionately benefit the poor—or at least not disproportionately benefit those who are better off. The aim of a benefit-incidence analysis (BIA) is to see whether it's the poor or better off who benefit disproportionately. A household survey is required to understand the patterns and use of household spending on health; it is also key to a benefit incidence analysis.

Service delivery indicators' study could bring about a better understanding of the performance and quality of care that health facilities provide. As of now, there is a gap. For example, are staffing levels adequate, do staff show up for work present, are drugs available, etc. A health facility bottleneck analysis could shed light on the constraints that impede performance and quality of care and how to resolve them.

Notes

1. Facility staff report that a general practitioner in public facilities earns a monthly salary of XAF 400,000 compared to one paid XAF 1.5 million employed by CNSS. At the Lambarene CHR hospital, incentive payments amount to 19 percent of total expenditure and 72 percent of the hospital's own revenue.

2. These regulations are Decree 00048/MSASSF/MTEPSPG (March 14, 2011) and Decree 01496/MSASSF/MTEPSPG (of November 14, 2011). They should have led MOHPH to implement regulations, but they were never issued.

3. In addition, the 20 percent copay will continue to be a direct source of revenues for providers.

4. La Forgia and Couttolenc, 2008 (Hospital Performance in Brazil—In search of Excellence); Couttolenc and Dmytraczenko, 2013 (UNICO Studies Series 2—Brazil's Primary Care Strategy).

5. Africa Health Forum: Finance and Capacity for Results. www.worldbank.org/afr/healthforum2013.

6. The UCS is a tax-funded health insurance scheme, targeting 47 million people who were not covered by the existing Civil Servant Medical Benefit Scheme (CSMBS) or Social Security Scheme (SSS).

7. However, in practice, the benefit of a progressive income tax is questionable due to tax evasions in many low-income countries (Kwon 2011).

8. This is Policy Note 19, written for the BPJS teams by Anna Monfert, GiZ, Annette Martin, Joint Learning Network, and Jack Langenbrunner, AusAID under the AusAID Health Systems Strengthening Project. This paper was written for the Informal Sector Conference in Yogjakarta September 29–October 2, 2103.

9. http://www.who.int/fctc/implementation/news/news_phl/en/.

Health Financing in the Republic of Gabon • http://dx.doi.org/10.1596/978-1-4648-0289-8

International Comparisons on Health Spending Levels

Table A.1 International Comparisons on Health Spending Levels, 2010

	GDP/capita	Total health expenditure (THE) % gross domestic product (GDP)	General government expenditure on health (GGHE) as % of THE	Social security funds as % of GGHE	Total expenditure on health/capita at exchange rate	Total expenditure on health/capita at Purchasing Power Parity (NCU per US$)	General government expenditure on health/cap x-rate	General government expenditure on health/cap Purchasing Power Parity (NCU per US$)
Upper middle income	7,289	6.3	49.5	6.8				
Sub-Saharan Africa (all income levels)	1,435							
Algeria	5,348	5	84	29	279	439	234	369
Angola	5,482	3	62	–	190	212	118	132
Botswana	7,238	5	56	:	384	872	216	491
Cameroon	1,167	5	34	3	59	120	20	40
Congo, Rep.	3,154	3	74	–	100	140	74	103
Côte d'Ivoire	1,244	7	27	7	88	144	24	40
Equatorial Guinea	24,036	5	54	:	1,138	1,432	618	777
Gabon	11,257	3	51	27	397	558	203	286
Ghana	1,605	5	57	:	83	106	47	61
Mauritius	8,120	5	49	:	444	784	217	384
Nigeria	1,555	6	31	:	94	161	29	50
Senegal	1,023	5	56	4	51	96	29	54
South Africa	7,508	9	48	:	645	982	309	470
Egypt, Arab Rep.	3,256	5	39	21	152	323	59	126
Morocco	2,902	:	33	25	190	340	64	114
Tunisia	4,237	7	59	56	297	686	175	405

Source: WHO National Health Accounts 2012 and WDI for GDP/capita.
Note: GDP = gross domestic product; GGHE = general government health expenditure; NCU = national currency unit; THE = total health expenditure.

Simulations

Table B.1 Simulation to Assess Additional Needs for Enrollment into CNAMGS

	2013	2014	2015	2016	2017	2018	2019	2020
Scale-up of population coverage	42%	43%	47%	57%	67%	74%	81%	88%
Full subsidy for GEF & informal sector	17,545,161,290	17,953,963,548	22,538,343,257	29,458,168,722	36,688,222,212	42,007,155,030	47,554,032,448	53,336,589,090
Full subsidy for GEF, partial (50%) subsidy for informal sector	17,545,161,290	17,953,963,548	20,455,317,078	24,129,267,000	27,963,318,000	30,846,911,930	33,849,700,331	36,975,672,191
Full subsidy for GEF, no subsidy for informal sector	17,545,161,290	17,953,963,548	18,372,290,899	18,800,365,277	19,238,413,788	19,686,668,829	20,145,368,213	20,614,755,292

Source: World Bank's estimates.
Note: GHS is government health spending; GDP is gross domestic product. Note (a): Inflation rate estimated at 2.3 percent, using the 2003–10 average as a reference point. GEF = Gabonais Economiquement Faibles.

Table B.2 Simulation to Assess Additional Fiscal Space

Background information: WB and IMF

IMF	Indicators (in billion)	2011	2012	2013	2014	2015	2016	2017	2018
	GDP, current dollar	18.78	18.4	19.97	21.11	22.12	23.5	25.22	27.25
	GDP, current NCU	8,852.07	9,382.44	9,922.34	10,404	10,794.2	11,362.2	12,092.2	12,960
	GDP, constant NCU	4,570.17	4,824.58	5,145.02	5,497.08	5,879.56	6,301.58	6,775.34	7,299.2
	GDP, PPP	25.89	27.81	30.06	32.65	35.63	38.98	42.78	47.03
WDI	Indicators (in billion)	2011	2012	2013	2014	2015	2016	2017	2018
	GDP, current dollar	18.76	18.38	N/A	N/A	N/A	N/A	N/A	N/A

Calculation using three scenarios

Formula: $(GHE\_t - GHE\_t\text{-}1)/[(GHE\_t + GHE\_t\text{-}1)/2] = elas * M = elas * (GDP\_t - GDP\_t\text{-}1)/[(GDP\_t + GDP\_t\text{-}1)/2]$

IMF		2011	2012	2013	2014	2015	2016	2017	2018
	GDP, constant NCU (in billions)	4,570.2	4,824.6	5,145.0	5,497.1	5,879.6	6,301.6	6,775.3	7,299.2
	M		0.1	0.1	0.1	0.1	0.1	0.1	0.1
WDI (assuming 4% growth rate)	GDP, constant NCU	4,570.2	4,824.6	5,017.6	5,218.3	5,427.0	5,644.1	5,869.8	6,104.6
	M		0.0	0.0	0.0	0.0	0.0	0.0	0.0
Government health expenditure, current NCU	Elasticity = 0.8	82.3	85.7	90.3	95.2	100.4	106.2	112.5	119.4
	Elasticity = 1.8	82.3	85.7	96.3	108.5	122.4	138.7	158.1	180.8
	Elasticity = 3	82.3	85.7	104.0	127.0	155.4	191.5	238.2	298.1
Government health expenditure, constant NCU	Elasticity = 0.8	82.3	85.7	88.5	91.3	94.2	97.2	100.3	103.5
	Elasticity = 1.8	82.3	85.7	92.0	98.7	106.0	113.7	122.0	131.0
	Elasticity = 3	82.3	85.7	96.5	108.5	122.1	137.3	154.5	173.8

Source: World Bank's estimates.

Note: IMF = International Monetary Fund; GDP = Gross Domestic Product; GHE = government health expenditure; IMF = International Monetary Fund; NCU = national currency unit; WDI = World Development Indicators.

Health and Revenue Benefits of Tobacco Excise Policies

Background

With a death toll of 6 million a year, tobacco kills more people than any other single cause—more than acquired immune deficiency syndrome (AIDS), malaria, and tuberculosis combined. Yet this only begins to describe the toll that tobacco takes: Tobacco snuffs out lives, cripples human potential, and creates greater poverty in countries, undermining the economic gains these countries have worked so hard to achieve during the past few decades.

However, while tobacco consumption in most developed countries is falling, in the developing world tobacco use is soaring. Although Sub-Saharan Africa has the lowest number of smokers per capita, this trend is changing rapidly. As a "green market," Sub-Saharan Africa is being targeted for market expansion. If nothing is done in the next 50 years, the number of smokers in Sub-Saharan Africa is expected to increase from about 77 million in 2010 to over 500 million.

Long before tobacco-related illness strikes, tobacco ensnares families into a vicious cycle of poverty that spans generations. Across the world, poor families with a tobacco user spend less on food, clothing, education, and water than poor families that do not use tobacco. The former also spend more on health because they are sick more often.

Tobacco control measures work and are highly cost effective. The WHO Framework Convention on Tobacco Control (FCTC), which Gabon signed in 2003 and ratified in 2009, identifies all the proven policies and measure that reduce tobacco use. Tobacco taxation, in particular, has proven an extremely potent tool for deterring tobacco use, especially among the young and poor. By ratifying the FCTC, Gabon committed to increase taxes to discourage tobacco consumption.

It is a common fiscal practice to submit certain "goods" with serious negative consequences for health or the environment to impose excise taxes to offset their social costs and discourage their consumption. Tobacco, alcohol and fuel are among them. Since the price elasticity of these substances is often less than one, tax increases also result in revenue increases.

To achieve its social/health/environmental policy objectives while also increasing revenue, excise taxes should follow a few principles: (i) the tax has to be high enough and maintained over a long enough period of time to increase a product's retail price; (ii) the tax needs to be indexed automatically to the nominal gross domestic product (GDP) growth rate or at least to the inflation rate. That way it progressively reduces the affordability of the targeted product; (iii) the tax structure needs to be simple—to reduce the possibility of gaming by industry, tax evasion and lack of transparency; (iv) tax structure should minimize the price differentials between low and high priced goods within a given category (for example cheap versus expensive cigarettes); and (v) tax structure should, when relevant, be indexed to reflect the good's level of harm based on each unit of consumption (that is liquors versus beer). Finally, as in the case of other consumption taxes (for example value added tax [VAT]), tax revenue/spending allocations should be pro-poor to offset any potential negative effects of the tax.

As tobacco taxes go up, the industry often reacts in a variety of ways, depending on the tobacco tax structure and the degree of competition. Some of these reactions include the following:

- The industry increases prices of that product above that required by the tax increase, so as to maintain total profits
- The industry "absorbs" some or the entire tax burden. Profits decline, but the retail price remains the same. If the tax is sufficiently high, this situation cannot be sustained indefinitely. Companies often use this tactic to demonstrate to the government that increased taxes do not reduce consumption
- Increase prices of some products, often the more expensive brands, above the tax increase, while keeping the prices of the cheaper brands at current market prices. In effect, the more expensive brand is subsidizing the less expensive brand, as people who buy the luxury brands are able to afford the higher prices, while the people who buy the less expensive brands will be adversely affected by the price increase if it took place. The industry is often concerned about losing market share on the less expensive brands thereby such a policy of cross-subsidizing can help them retain the market share
- Front loading production before the tax increase goes into effect in order to sell cigarettes at the old prices. This often results in a temporary reduction in revenue reduction as a ploy to scare the government.

If the government persists and the tax structure is adequate, both the health and revenue goals can be reached. No country has yet lost revenue after a sound tax increase.

Gabon Situation

Since 2011, approximately 11 percent of the adult population are smokers and about 20 percent of the male population.

Gabon tobacco tax structure is as follows: (i) an excise ad valorem tax, currently calculated at 30 percent of ex-factory price; and (ii) a value added tax of 18 percent (of the retail sales price (RSP)) applied to all goods. RSP = ex-factory price + Excise tax + wholesale and retail distribution margins + value added tax. These two taxes add up to an effective total tax share of 34.8 percent of retail sales prices (WHO Tobacco Free Initiative). The last excise tax increase took place in 2011 and has remained unchanged since then. In recent years, the collection of tobacco excise taxes fluctuated around 0.03 percent of GDP.

An analysis shows that the 2011 tobacco excise tax increase did not result in a retail price increase on the best-selling brand. Today, as in 2011, the best-selling brand remains at XAF 1,000 per pack of 20 cigarettes. No positive health outcome should be expected of the tax increase on the smokers of this brand. On the contrary, as Gabon's growth in GDP goes up, cigarettes will become more affordable. Then it's possible more people will start smoking or increase the number of cigarettes they consume.

Potential for Tobacco Tax Reform

If, in 2011, the Government had chosen a moderate three-year policy of tax rate increases—instead of maintaining tobacco excise rates at a constant level, the results in terms of sales, excise revenue and smoking prevalence would have been more positive.

We modeled tax increases of 50 percent in 2011, 60 percent in 2012 and 65 percent in 2013.[1] The results appear in figure C.1. If the modelled tax increases had been implemented, Gabon could have:

- Reduced the volume of cigarette sales by almost one-quarter
- Reduced the prevalence of smoking from around 11 percent of the adult population in 2011 to 9.58 percent in 2013
- Expanded its tobacco excise revenues to 136 percent in 2013, totaling XAF 5,600 million (increasing from 0.03 percent to 0.06 percent of GDP)
- More than doubled total tobacco fiscal revenues (including value added taxes) and would have reached almost 12 billion or would have gone from 0.07 to 0.12 percent of GDP.

Then, as seen in many other countries, Gabon could have obtained the doubly beneficial effect of decreasing the prevalence of smoking and its associated burden of diseases and expanded fiscal revenues from tobacco by almost 0.05 percent of GDP.

Figure C.1 Simulation of Outcomes of an Excise Tax Increase on Tobacco Products

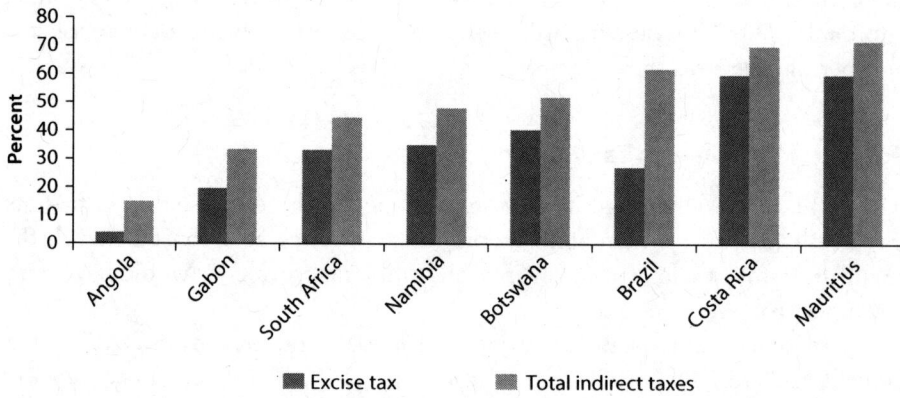

	2011	Year 1	Year 2	Year 3
Consupt (index)	100	96.3	84.9	76.9
Excise tax revenue index	100	157.6	202.3	236.2
Total revenue index	100	131.5	169.5	203.1

Source: World Bank's calculations.

Figure C.2 Taxes as Percentage of the Most Popular Brand in a Set of Upper-Middle-Income Countries, 2012

Source: WHO Global Tobacco Control Report III, 2013.

Gabon has room to increase taxes as a percentage of the retail price of its cigarettes. To demonstrate, figure C.2 displays total indirect taxes as a percentage of price of the most-popular brand. It also displays excise taxes as a percentage of the price in a set of upper-middle-income countries in Africa and Latin America. Angola and Gabon are the only ones with pure ad valorem taxes. In contrast, Costa Rica and Brazil have a combination of specific and ad valorem rates in their excise systems. The rest of the sample has a purely specific system. Compared to this group of countries with similar GDP per capita, Gabon had one of the lowest indirect taxes in 2012 as a percentage of the price of the most-popular brand. Brazil also has a relatively low excise tax, but it's VAT and other indirect taxes are high enough to ensure a high price and a high overall tax rate on cigarettes.

The objectives of applying excise taxes to tobacco products are to raise prices in relationship to personal disposable income, to reduce consumption and

Figure C.3 Ratio of 100 Packs of the Most Popular Brand to GDP Per Capita (Percentage) in a Set of Upper-Middle-Income Countries, 2012

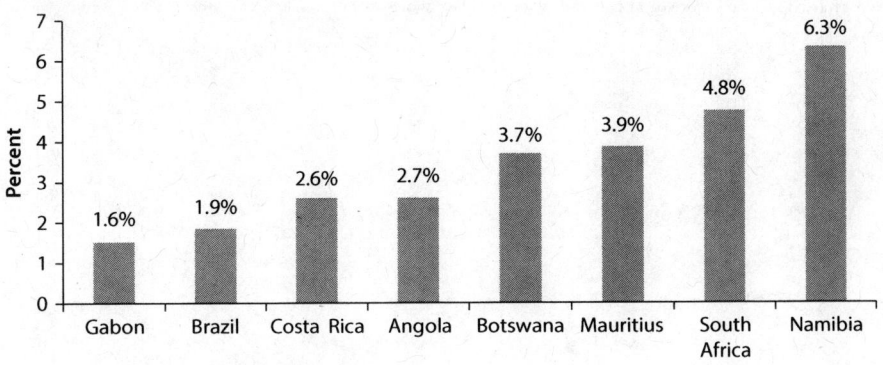

Source: WHO Global Tobacco Control Report III, 2013.

support quitting. Another way to analyze a tobacco excise tax policy is to view the relationship of price of tobacco products to GDP per capita. Figure C.3 presents the ratio of 100 packs of the most popular brand of cigarettes in 2012 to GDP per capita in the same set of upper-middle-income countries. Again, Gabon shows the lowest relationship of prices to disposable income compared to these other countries. As a result, cigarettes are, on average, very affordable in Gabon. This situation supports heavy consumption among smokers and easy access to cigarettes by youth. Gabon's tobacco excise policy could make tobacco products less affordable, which could lead to lower consumption and higher fiscal revenues.

Given the preceding analysis, we recommend that the Gabonese government consider reforming and increasing its tobacco taxes with the goal of reducing consumption. That would make it less likely that Gabon would join countries facing a tobacco "epidemic." It should also improve health outcomes in the short and medium terms and increase revenue from a nonproductive sector.

Note

1. Assuming the following parameters of the cigarette market:
   - Average starting price per pack of 750 XFA
   - Cigarette price elasticity: -0.5
   - Income elasticity: 0.6
   - Industry passing the tax increases on to the consumer through increased prices (average retail price 850, 1100 & 1350 XAF).

Short and Medium Term Reform Consideration

Table D.1 Short and Medium Term Reform Consideration

Diagnostics	Recommendations	
	Short term (1–3 years)	Medium term (3–5 years)
Health service delivery		
Poor access to public health programs and outreach	Intensify strategy for public health programs and outreach	Implement various models of outreach and community based programs.
Poor access to primary health care	Diagnose the problem in-depth and develop strategy to improve the access to health services	Improve access to primary health care services, with appropriate emergency care referrals, etc. with special emphasis to rural and poorer regions.
Poor quality of health care	Diagnose the problem in-depth and develop strategy to improve the quality of health services	Test innovative ways to incentivize and improve service delivery performance
Human resources		
Inequitable distribution of human resources	Diagnose the problem in-depth and develop strategy to improve the staffing distribution to rural areas and to underserved areas	Test innovative ways to incentivize redistribution
Weak staff accountability	Develop mechanisms to improve accountability, for example technical audits, reporting, etc.	Pilot test some accountability mechanisms
Low staff performance	Develop mechanisms to improve staff performance, for example bonus/payments based on performance, etc.	Pilot test some performance based payment mechanism
Drugs		
	There is an existing policy that drugs can only be available at health facilities in the presence of pharmacists. Many health facilities therefore do not have drugs. This policy needs to be reviewed and its practicality assessed.	
Areas for efficiency gain		
Too high a budget share for capital investment	Need a capital investment rationalization plan based on need	
Too many hospital beds and underutilization	Need a hospital rationalization plan based on need	

table continues next page

Table D.1 Short and Medium Term Reform Consideration *(continued)*

Diagnostics	Recommendations	
	Short term (1–3 years)	*Medium term (3–5 years)*
Bypassing of PHC in favor of hospitals	review the PHC quality of care – consider conducting a service delivery performance assessment	Reconsider strategy to improve quality of care: including HRH, drugs, etc.
CNAMGS		
Low financial protection		
	Develop strategy for scaling up and incentivizing enrollment (including considering challenges for adverse selection)	Increase enrollment into the NHIP/ CNAMGS
	Review the current mechanisms for identification of the poor, and consider refinement	Identify those who are the poor and provide free coverage
	Develop a strategy for identification and incentivizing enrollment of the informal sector (including consideration of adverse selection challenges)	Identify those who are in the informal sector, and suggest ways to improve incentive for their enrollment
	Review the situation on household spending (OOP) on health	Reconsider who should be charged copayments, poor, informal sector workers, formal sector, etc.
	Review the situation of balance billing and pricing amounts with private sector	Reconsider pricing and performance based contract with the private sector, and the balance billing situation
Unknown financial sustainability of the CNAMGS scheme		
	Cost out the benefits package using actuarial methods	
	Conduct actuarial analysis, and estimate premiums (pro-rated) by income levels	
		Consider pooling of resources of the various schemes under CNAMGS, and consider cross-subsidization between schemes
		Reconsider sources of financing: general taxes, indirect taxes, earmarked taxes, payroll taxes.
internally generated revenue	Review the situation of internally generated revenue, its reporting and enforcement of the policy	Reconsider policy
Efficiency		
- Claims management	Develop strategy for eclaims, including costing of the eclaims package and readiness at CNAMGS and at service facilities	Introduce phase 1 of the electronic claims management (eclaims)

table continues next page

Table D.1 Short and Medium Term Reform Consideration *(continued)*

Diagnostics	Recommendations	
	Short term (1–3 years)	*Medium term (3–5 years)*
- Provider payment mechanism	Review the provider payment mechanisms and its effect on costs and on service use	
	Develop strategy for refinement of the provider payment mechanism.	Refine the provider payment mechanism so that it improves efficiency, including capitation, case mix.
- Population identification mechanism	Refine the mechanism for identification of the poor under the CNAMGS	
- Contractual pricing for services and drugs	Reconsider pricing for drugs (how do they fare in comparison to international reference pricing) under the CNAMGS package	
	Reconsider pricing for services (public and nonpublic) under the CNAMGS package. Who should pay for staff? What can be done about the balance billing in private sector service pricing?	
	claims for drugs has been going up under CNAMGS. Is this a result of drug prescribing behavior?	Refine strategy, including possibility of bundling services and drugs under reimbursement
Cost containment	• Improve audits for fraud prevention.	• Improve gatekeeping to reduce unnecessary use of services or reduce the use of primary services at higher-level facilities
Administrative reforms	• Use data to support evidence-based policies and systems.	• • Review and integrate the NHIS beneficiaries database with the claims reimbursement database.
Provider payment reforms	• Review the current fee-for-service, which separates services from drug reimbursement.	• Implement payment systems that encourage efficiency, quality, cost-effective service utilization, and better coordination across the continuum of care. Options include the appropriate mix of capitation, other bundled payment systems, blended payment systems, various managed care approaches, and modern pay-for-performance systems.
	• Review the pricing structure under the fee-for-payment system.	
	• Review incentives and their effect on utilization patterns, including drug use.	
Health financing		
	• Develop a health financing strategy.	
	• Support demand-side financing initiatives.	

table continues next page

Table D.1 Short and Medium Term Reform Consideration (continued)

Diagnostics	Recommendations	
	Short term (1–3 years)	Medium term (3–5 years)
	• Reduce fragmentation in health financing flows and funds.	
	• Improve expenditure management and tracking systems and support NHAs.	
		• Firm up plans for devolution of financing functions.
NHIS eligibility changes	• Focus on the poor (support and scale up targeting mechanism).	
	• Consider refining the eligibility for the exempt group.	
	• Develop incentives to encourage enrollment.	
NHIS benefits package	• Reassess the basic benefits package on the basis of its cost effectiveness, financial protection, and financial sustainability.	
	• Consider developing cost sharing, at least for certain services and for certain beneficiary groups such as the non-poor.	
	• Improve coordination with vertical public health programs.	
NHIS revenue	• Assess the situation under the earmarked taxes and levies to finance the GEF scheme.	
	Conduct a feasibility of tobacco and alcohol taxes	• Introduce tobacco and alcohol taxes.
	• Consider exemption of beneficiaries based on means testing.	
	Create further incentives to encourage enrollment of informal sector workers.	
	• Consider income-related premiums.	
	• Assess the role and appropriate level for the reserve fund.	

Source: World Bank.
Note: CNAMGS = Caisse Nationale d'Assurance Maladie et de Garantie Sociale; GEF = Gabonais Economiquement Faibles; NHA = National Health Accounts; NHIP = National Health Insurance Program; OOP = out-of-pocket; PHC = primary health care.

Bibliography

Alexander, C. A., G. Busch, and K. Stringer. 2003. "Implementing and Interpreting a Data Envelopment Analysis Model to Assess the Efficiency of Health Systems in Developing Countries." *IMA Journal of Management Mathematics* 14 (1): 49–63.

Axco Global Statistics: Gabon Profile. London, 2014.

Boidin, B. 2011. "La 'bonne gouvernance'et les pays en développement: le cas des politiques de santé au Gabon."https://papyrus.bib.umontreal.ca/xmlui/handle/1866/5130.

Bokhari, F., Y. Gai, and P. Gottret. 2007. "Government Health Expenditure and Health Outcomes." *Health Economics* 16 (3): 257–73.

Business Monitor International: Gabon Pharmaceuticals & Healthcare Report 2014. http://www.businessmonitor.com.

Caisse Nationale d'Assurance Maladie et de Garantie Sociale (CNAMGS): Directive No. 001/08-DG. http://itemcpclab.pro/cnamgs/.

Center for Global Development. 2007. "Does the IMF Constrain Health Spending in Poor Countries?" Report of the Working Group on IMF programs and Health Spending, Washington, DC.

Cetrangolo, O., J. P. Jimenez, and R. R. Del Castillo. 2010. "Rigidities and Fiscal Space in Latin America: A Comparative Case Study." Economic Development Division, United Nations.

Direction Générale de la Statistique et des Études Economiques, CNAMGS: Recensement des Gabonais Economiquement Faibles. 2008. Gabon, 2009.

The Economist. 2013. "Gabon Country Report." Economic Intelligence Unit, London.

Estache, A., M. Gonzalez, and L. Trujillo. 2007. "Government Expenditures in Education, Health and Infrastructure: A Naïve Look at Levels, Outcomes and Efficiency." World Bank Policy Research Working Paper, World Bank, Washington, DC.

Filmer, D., and L. Pritchett. 1997. "Child Mortality and Public Spending on Health: How Much Does Money matter?" Policy Research Working Paper 1864, World Bank, Washington, DC.

———. 1999. "The Impact of Public Spending on Health: Does Money matter?" *Social Science and Medicine* 49 (10): 1309–23.

Fleisher, L., and A. Tandon. Forthcoming. "The Macro-Fiscal Context of Universal Coverage in Vietnam." Health Insurance Review of Vietnam, World Bank, Washington, DC.

Gertler, P., and C. Vermeersch. 2012. "Using Performance Incentives to Improve Health Outcomes." Policy Research Working Paper WPS6100, World Bank, Washington, DC.

Gottret, P., and G. Schieber. 2006. *Health Financing Revisited: A Practitioner's Guide.* Washington, DC: World Bank.

Gottret, P., G. Schieber, and W. Raters. 2008. *Good Practices in Health Financing.* Washington, DC: World Bank.

Government of Gabon. 2012. Growth and Poverty Reduction Strategy Paper.

Gupta, S., and M. Verhoeven. 2001. "The Efficiency of Government Expenditures: Experiences from Africa." *Journal of Policy Modeling* 23: 433–67.

Hanson, K., K. Ranson, V. Oliveira-Cruz, and A. Mills. 2003. "Expanding Access to Health Interventions: A Framework for Understanding the Constraints to Scaling-up." *Journal of International Development* 15 (1): 1–14.

Heller, P. 2006. "The Prospect of Creating Fiscal Space for the Health Sector." *Health Policy and Planning* 21 (2): 75–79.

Herrera, S., and G. Pang. 2005. "Efficiency of Public Spending in Developing Countries: An Efficiency Frontier Approach." World Bank Policy Research Working Paper 3645, World Bank, Washington, DC.

Humphreys, G. 2013. "Gabon Gets Everyone under One Social Health Insurance Roof." *Bull World Health Organ* 91: 318–19. World Health Organization. http://dx.doi.org/10.2471/BLT.13.020513.

Inoua, Aboubacar, and Laurent Musango. 2013. "La Caisse nationale d'assurance maladie et de garantie sociale du Gabon: Un chemin vers la couverture universelle." World Health Organization, Issue 17, Special Issue, Health Financing in the African Region, African Health Monitor, July 2013. http://www.aho.afro.who.int/sites/default/files/ahm/reports/631/ahm1705.pdf.

Institute for Health Metrics and Evaluation: Global Burden of Disease Study 2010. Seattle.

International Medical Alliance (IMEDA). 2004. Le Systëme de Santé au Gabon—Un Besoin de Solidarité Nationale. Rapport de Mission.

International Monetary Fund: Gabon: 2006 Article IV Consultation-Staff Report, IMF, Washington, DC.

Keen, M., and M. Mansour. 2008. "Revenue Mobilization in Sub-Saharan Africa: Key Challenges for Globalization." Paper presented at the conference "Globalization and Revenue Mobilization," Abuja, Nigeria.

Keen, M., and A. Simone. 2004. "Tax Policy in Developing Countries: Some Lessons from the 1990s and Some Challenges Ahead." In *Helping Countries Develop: The Role of Fiscal Policy*, edited by S. Gupta, B. Clements, and G. Inschauste. Washington, DC: IMF.

Kutzin, Joseph, Cheryl Cashin, and Melitta Jakab. 2010. *Implementing Health Financing Reform: Lessons from Countries in Transition.* European Observatory. World Health Organization, Brussels, Belgium.

Kwon, Soonman. 2009. "Thirty Years of National Health Insurance in South Korea: Lessons for Achieving Universal Health Care Coverage." *Health Policy and Planning* 24: 63-71.

La Forgia, G., and B. Couttolenc. 2008. (Hospital Performance in Brazil—In search of Excellence); Couttolenc and Dmytraczenko, 2013 (UNICO Studies Series 2—Brazil's Primary Care Strategy).

Langenbrunner, John, Cheryl Cashin, and Sheila O'Dougherty, eds. 2009. *Designing and Implementing Health Care Provider Payment Systems: How-to Manual*. World Bank and USAID.

http://books.google.com/books?hl=en&lr=&id=vyJP_GvskEIC&oi=fnd&pg=PR5&dq=langenbrunner+2009&ots=KTw8whkQ4s&sig=KfpS3CB640izFSwcq83m9ZOIPls#v=onepage&q=langenbrunner%202009&f=false.

Li, Cheng, Xuan Yu, James R. G. Butler, Vasoontara Yiengprugsawan, and Min Yu. 2011. "Moving Towards Universal Health Insurance in China: Performance, Issues and Lessons from Thailand." *Social Science & Medicine* 73: 359–66.

Lieberman, A., and A. Wagstaff. 2009. *Health Financing and Delivery in Vietnam*. Washington, DC: World Bank.

Maino, R., and J. Troujas-Bernate. 2013. "Gabon's Priority: Use Resources to Become Emerging Economy." IMF Survey Magazine: Countries and Regions, International Monetary Fund, African Department. https://www.imf.org/external/pubs/ft/survey/so/2013/car022813c.htm.

Mbeng-Mendou, J. P. 2011. "Innovative Financing of Health Care in Gabon." Presentation to the Prince Mahidol Award Conference (PMAC) Conference, Bangkok.

Ministère de la Planification, de la Programmation du Développement et de l'Aménagement du Territoire, Direction Générale de la Statistique et des Études Economiques. 2005. "Enquête Générale sur l'Évolution de la Pauvreté." Libreville, Gabon.

Ministère de la Santé, des Affaires Sociales, de la Solidarité, et de la Famille. 2010. "Plan National de Développement Sanitaire 2011–2015." Libreville, Gabon.

———. 2011. "Normes du Secteur de la Santé." Libreville, Gabon.

Ministère de la Santé Publique. 1998. "Plan National d'Action Sanitaire (1998–2000)." Libreville, Gabon.

———. 2005. "États Généraux de la Santé, Les Actes." Libreville, Gabon.

———. 2010a. "Plan National de Development de la Santé." Libreville, Gabon.

———. 2010b. "Politique Nationale de Santé 2010." Libreville, Gabon.

Ministère de la Santé Publique: Cellule d'Observation de la Santé Publique. 2007. "Tableau de Bord Général de la Santé Publique 2005." Libreville, Gabon.

Ministère de la Santé Publique et CREDES. 2005a. "Realisation de l'Étude Stratégique du Secteur de la Santé et Finalisation de la Carte Sanitaire." Rapport Final, Tome I—Analyse de Situation. Libreville, Gabon.

———. 2005b. "Realisation de l'Étude Stratégique du Secteur de la Santé et Finalisation de la Carte Sanitaire." Rapport Final, Tome II—Plan National de Développement Sanitaire 2006–2010. Libreville, Gabon.

Ministère de la Santé Publique et de l'Hygiène Publique. 2008. "Carte Sanitaire." Libreville, Gabon.

Ministère de l'Economie, de l'Emploi et du Développement Durable, Ministère de la Santé. 2001. "Enquête Démographique et de Santé 2000." Libreville, Gabon.

———. 2013. "Enquête Démographique et de Santé 2012." Libreville, Gabon.

Ministère de l'Economie, de l'Emploi et du Développement Durable, Ministère du Budget, des Comptes Publics et de la Fonction Publique. 2012. "Rapport de Programmation Macroéconomique et Budgétaire 2013–2015, Annexe du Projet de Loi de Finances." Libreville, Gabon.

Ministère des Affaires Etrangères (France), Direction Générale de la Coopération et du Développement. 2002. "Evaluation de la Coopération Française dans le Secteur Sante au Gabon (1990–2001)." Paris.

Monfert, Anna, Annette Martin, and Jack Langenbrunner. Policy Note 19, Informal Sector Conference in Yogjakarta September 29–October 2, 2103.

Musango, Laurent, and Aboubacar Inoua. 2010. "Assurance Maladie Obligatoire au Gabon: Un Atout Pour le Bien Être de la Population." World Health Report, Background Paper, 16. http://www.who.int/healthsystems/topics/financing/healthreport/GabonNo16FINAL.pdf?

Nkale Bougha Obouna, E. 2011. "Pauvreté, santé et genre au Gabon." http://www.theses.fr/2011BOR40021.

Okwero, P., A. Tandon, S. Sparkes, J. Mclaughlin, and J. Hoogeveen. 2010. *Fiscal Space for Health in Uganda*. Africa Human Development Series. Washington, DC: World Bank.

Organisation for Economic Co-operation and Development (OECD). 2012. "Pharmaceutical expenditure." In *Health at a Glance: Europe 2012*. OECD Publishing. http://dx.doi.org/10.1787/9789264183896-55-en.

Palafox, B. 2009. "Good Health at Low Cost Revisited (Chapter 8)." In *Health at Low Cost*. London: London School of Hygiene and Tropical Medicine.

Pande, A., A. Leive, M. Smitz, P. Eozenou, and E. Ozcelik. 2013. *Macro Fiscal Context and Health Financing Fact Sheet*. Washington, DC: World Bank.

Park, M., T. Braun, G. Carrin, and D. B. Evans. 2007. "Provider Payments and Cost Containment. Lessons from OECD Countries." *Technical Briefs for Policy Makers*. Geneva, WHO.

Republic of Gabon, Ministry of Health and Public Hygiene. 2010. National Health Development Plan 2011–2015, December. http://www.mindbank.info/item/2552. (République Gabonaise Union—Travail—Justice. Ministère de la Santé, des Affaires Sociales, de la Solidarite et de la Famille, December 2010. Plan National De Développement Sanitaire 2011–2015.)

République Gabonaise Union—Travail—Justice. 2001. Enquête Démographique et de Santé 2012 (Gabon Demographic Health Survey 2000). Ministère de la Planification, de la Programmation du Développement et de l'Aménagement du Territoire, Direction Générale de la Statistique, et des Études Économiques, Fonds des Nations Unies pour la Population, ORC Macro, June.

———. 2009. Annuaire Statistique du Gabon 2001–2007. Ministère du Développement, de la Performance République Gabonaise Publique, de la Prospective et de la Statistique, July. http://www.stat-gabon.org/documents/PDF/Donnees%20stat/Compteannuaire/Ann09.pdf.

———. 2013. Enquête Démographique et de Santé 2012 (Gabon Demographic Health Survey 2012). Ministère de l'Économie, de l'Emploi et du Développement Durable, Ministère de la Santé, Direction Générale de la Statistique, Libreville, ICF International, Calverton, Maryland, USA, April.

Sachs, J. 2001. "Macroeconomics and Health: Investing in Health for Economic Development." Report of the Commission on Macroeconomics and Health, WHO, Geneva.

Saleh, Karima. 2012. *The Health Sector in Ghana: A Comprehensive Assessment*. Directions in Development. Washington, DC: World Bank.

Schieber, George, Cheryl Cashin, Karima Saleh, and Rouselle Lavado. 2012. *Health Financing in Ghana*. Directions in Development. Washington, DC: World Bank.

Tandon, A., and C. Cashin. 2010. "Assessing Public Expenditure on Health from a Fiscal Space Perspective, Health, Nutrition, and Population (HNP)." Discussion Paper, World Bank, Washington, DC.

Tandon, A., C. J. L. Murray, J. Lauer, and D. B. Evans. 2000. "Measuring Overall Health System Performance for 191 Countries." Global Programme on Evidence for Health (GPE) Discussion Paper No. 30, World Health Organization, Geneva.

Tangcharoensathien, Viroj, Walaiporn Patcharanarumol, Por Ir, Syed Mohamed Aljunid, Ali Ghufron Mukti, Kongsap Akkhavong, Eduardo Banzon, Dang Boi Huong, Hasbullah Thabrany, and Anne Mills. 2011. "Health-financing Reforms in Southeast Asia: Challenges in Achieving Universal Coverage." *The Lancet* 377: 863-73.

Taskforce on Innovative International Financing for Health Systems. 2009. "Constraints to Scaling Up and Costs: Working Group 1 Report." International Health Partnership, Geneva (accessed April 27, 2010),

http://www.internationalhealthpartnership.net//CMS_files/documents/working_group_1_-_report_EN.pdf.

———. 2010. "Constraints to Scaling Up the Health Millennium Development Goals: Costing and Financial Gap Analysis." Working Group 1 Report, Geneva.

United Nations. 2013. "Gouvernance du financement de la santé mondiale: enjeux et perspectives africains." http://www.africa21.org/wp/wp-content/uploads/2013/02/Africa-21-note-n%C2%B02-Gouvernance-du-financement-de-la-sant%C3%A9-mondiale_-enjeux-et-perspectives-africains.pdf.

United Nations Development Programme (UNDP). 2010. "Objectifs du Millénaire Pour le Développent—Troisième Rapport National." UNDP, Gabon.

———. 2013. "Human Development Report 2013." UNDP, New York.

———. 2014. Human Development Report. http://hdr.undp.org/en.

United Nations Joint Programme on AIDS (UNAIDS). 2013. "Global Report 2013." UNAIDS, Geneva.

United Nations Population Fund (UNFPA). 2010. "Rapport Final de l'Enquête sur l'Evaluation des Besoins en Matière des soins Obstétricaux et Néonataux d'Urgence (SONU) au Gabon." UNFPA, Gabon.

Wagstaff, Adam, Magnus Lindelow, Gao Lun, Xu Ling, and Qian Juncheng. 2009. "Extending Health Insurance to the Rural Population: An Impact Evaluation of China's New Cooperative Medical Scheme." *Journal of Health Economics* 28: 1-19.

World Bank. 2005. *Gabon Country Assistance Strategy*. Washington, DC: World Bank.

———. 2006. "Diagnostique de la Pauvreté. Réduction de la Pauvreté et Gestion Economique, Région Afrique Sub-Saharienne." World Bank, Washington, DC.

———. 2007. "Does the IMF Constrain Health Spending in Poor Countries? Evidence and an Agenda for Action." Report of the CGD Working Group on IMF Programs and Health Spending, Washington, DC.

———. 2009a. "Assessing Fiscal Space for Health in Nepal." HNP Discussion Paper, South Asia Region, World Bank, Washington, DC.

———. 2009b. *Giving More Weight to Health: Assessing Fiscal Space for Health in Indonesia*. Washington, DC: World Bank.

World Bank. 2012. "Gabon Public Expenditure Review Better Management of Public Finance to Achieve Millennium Development Goals." Department for Poverty Reduction and Economic Management 3, Africa Region, Report No. 62548-GA. http://www-wds.worldbank.org/external/default/WDSContentServer/WDSP/IB/20 12/08/23/000386194_20120823014215/Rendered/PDF /625480ESW0GRAY0C0disclosed080210120.pdf.

———. 2012a. *Gabon Country Partnership Strategy*. Washington, DC: World Bank.

———. 2012b. "Gabon Public Expenditure Review—Better Management of Public Finance to Achieve Millennium Development Goals." Report No. 62548-GA, World Bank, Washington, DC.

———. 2013a. *Africa Health Forum: Finance and Capacity for Results. Chapter on Results-Based Financing for Health*. Washington, DC: World Bank.

———. 2013b. *Analyse de croissance du Gabon*. Draft Report.

———. 2013c. *World Development Indicators*. Washington, DC: World Bank. http://data. worldbank.org/data-catalog/world-development-indicators.

World Health Organization (WHO). 2003. "How Much Should Countries Spend on Health?" Discussion Paper #2, Department "Health System Financing, Expenditure and Resource Allocation" (FER) Cluster "Evidence and Information for Policy" (EIP), WHO. http://www.who.int/health_financing/en/how_much_should_dp_03_2.pdf.

———. 2010a. "Factsheet of Health Statistics." Gabon Report, Regional Office for Africa, WHO, Brazzaville.

———. 2010b. "Gabon Health Statistics Profile 2010." WHO, Brazzaville.

———. 2012a. "Gabon Country Profile: Maternal, Newborn and Child Survival," March. http://www.childinfo.org/files/maternal/DI%20Profile%20-%20Gabon.pdf

———. 2012b. *National Health Accounts Database*. Geneva: WHO. http://apps.who.int/ nha/database/PreDataExplorer.aspx?d=1.

———. 2012c. "Profil Analytique Gabon 2012: Observatoire de la santé en Afrique." WHO, Brazzaville.

———. 2012d. "State of Health Financing in the Africa Region." Discussion Paper for the Inter-ministerial Conference: Achieving Results and Value for Money in Health, WHO, Tunis.

———. 2013. "Global Tobacco Control Report III, 2013." WHO, Geneva.

WHO, UNICEF, UNFPA and The World Bank estimates. "Trends in Maternal Mortality: 1990 to 2010." In WHO. Maternal and perinatal health profile. http://www.who.int/ maternal_child_adolescent/epidemiology/profiles/maternal/gab.pdf.

Xu, Ke, Priyanka Saksena, Matthew Jowett, Chandika Indikadahena, Joe Kutzin, and David Evans. 2010. "Exploring the Thresholds of Health Expenditure for Protection against Financial risk." World Health Report, Background Paper, 19, Health Systems Financing: The Path to Universal Coverage, WHO, Geneva, Switzerland.